Great Indian Tribes

by
Daniel Jacobson

Illustrations
by
Don Spaulding

HAMMOND®
INCORPORATED

To
Nora and Bel Abbey,
Joyce, Wilma, and Myrna
and the
Koasati of Bayou Blue.

Contents

Introduction

American Indian Tribes: The Beginnings

Haida, Zuni, Creek, Crow, Yaqui, Aztec, Nez Perce, Mandan, Pomo—the American Indian tribes! The hunters, the seed gatherers, the fishermen, the farmers. The "primitive" and the "civilized." What do we really know of their lives? How much of their past and present do we really understand? What do we know of their origins and migrations, their social and political organization, their religious ceremonies, their everyday life? What do we know of their changing ways as a result of contacts with each other, with Europeans, with Americans? What do we know of their numbers, their reservation life, their present-day conditions?

STRANGE NOTIONS

Strange notions, for example, have long been held concerning the origin of the Indians. Egypt, Wales, West Africa, the mythical islands of Atlantis and Mu, and northeastern, southeastern, and southwestern Asia have all been cited as possible points of origin. Korea, China, and the Greece of Alexander the Great's day have all had their individual advocates. There have been those who have passionately defended the notion that the Indians were descended from the so-called "ten lost tribes" of Israel. James Adair's famous volume, the *History of the American Indians,* published in London in 1775, was based upon such a notion. Edward King, Viscount Kingsborough, a passionate lover of Mexican antiquities, even added the time dimension. The Hebrews, he pointed out, had reached North American shores via the sea in the 5th century B.C. *The Articles of Faith for the Book of Mormon,* part of the creed of the Church of Latter-Day Saints to this very day, supports the Hebrew or "ten lost tribes" notion of American Indian origins.

Meanwhile archaeologists, geologists, geographers, and other specialists, scholars primarily concerned with American Indian origins, have continued through the use of new devices and techniques to push the time for man's arrival in North America further and further back. As early as 1926, through Folsom Point discoveries made in New Mexico and subsequently on the Great Plains further east, it was learned that man had occupied the American earth at least 10,000 years ago. When stone implements and hearths, associated with bison, mammoth, and mastodon remains, were found in Sandia Cave, New Mexico (1935), man's presence in North America was pushed even further back — to perhaps 15,000 years ago. More recently radio-carbon dating has established the possibility of man's presence in Venezuela over 15,000 years ago, and at La Jolla, California, over 20,000 years ago. Even earlier radio-carbon dates have been reported for Santa Rosa Island (over 30,000 years ago) and for the Texas Street site, San Diego (over 38,000 years ago). There are scholars (they are very few indeed), therefore, who would push man's beginnings in North America back to the earliest days of the last continental glaciation to the so-called Wisconsin Ice Age and even earlier. Texas Street, if valid, is pre-Wisconsin.

The "strange notions" concerning Indian origins are obviously no longer tenable. Radio-carbon dates (indicating man's association with the flora and fauna of the day), our growing knowledge of migrating man and of Mongoloid man in particular, the distribution of ice sheets during the Wisconsin glaciation, and perhaps even linguistic considerations, all brought into focus, tend to lend support to the movement by man over the Alaskan or Bering Land Bridge. The earliest migrants, moving north from the Ordos Desert of Mongolia along the Asiatic seacoast and east through Kamchatka, pushed into Alaska *on land* perhaps 40,000 years ago. Later migrations, perhaps 25,000 years ago, orig-

inating in Asia's deep interior, may well have used the Lena River to provide access to the Arctic littoral and ultimately to the land bridge. The migrants in keen pursuit of their food supply — small animals, wild berries and fruits, and the meat of the old bison or mammoth when available — moved north of the Brooks Range, east along the Arctic coast, and south through the non-glaciated valley of the Mackenzie River. Generations of humankind were involved in the migrations. But the descendants of the earliest migrants did establish their campsites on the American plains, perhaps over 20,000 years ago.

EARLY DIFFERENTIATION OF CULTURES

By 10,000 B.C. Indian groups had already evolved many different life patterns across the continent. On the Great Plains the Big Game Hunters were bringing mammoth and bison to earth with spears carrying Folsom or Clovis points. In the Pacific Northwest Old Cordillerans, using so-called Cascade points, were likewise hunters, but they were able to supplement their food supply through salmon fishing, and by collecting wild roots, nuts and berries. In the Great Basin (the pluvial lake country of Utah and Nevada) the carriers of the Desert tradition learned to subsist on aquatic birds, fish, and the meat of the ground sloth and other animals. They learned also to grind seeds on milling stones and to make sandals and baskets.

The Big Game Hunters were not confined to the American West; they were also flourishing in the American East. With the retreat of the continental glaciers Big Game Hunters had moved into southwestern Michigan, where the mastodon became a favorite target, while other Big Game Hunters were busy between Alabama and Massachusetts.

Nor were the carriers of the Desert tradition idle. Migrants from the Great Basin had pushed south into Mexico, into Central America, and even into the remote corners of South America. Radio-carbon dates record the use of milling stones in distant Tierra del Fuego not less than 8,000 years ago. The American Indians then had by that date occupied all of the Americas.

THE AGRICULTURAL REVOLUTION

The carriers of the Desert tradition were not always on the move. They stopped to make camp where water was available, where hunting was good, and where plant collecting could furnish a good portion of their diet. Southern Tamaulipas and the hot and dry Tehuacán Valley of Puebla were particularly well blessed with a wide variety of plant foods; Desert peoples had already settled in both prior to 9000 B.C. Casual observations of wild plants made through the centuries may have kindled the idea of planting seeds in both areas. Gourds, pumpkins, runner beans and chili peppers were already being planted in Tamaulipas between 7000 and 5500 B.C. During the same period sometime-farmers in the Tehuacán Valley were planting avocado, the ever present chili pepper, and the amaranth. It was, of course, an incipient agriculture. The planted crops (field and tree) supplied perhaps only ten to twenty percent of the food supply during those early years. By 1500 B.C. maize, sunflowers, lima beans and squash had been added to the crop assemblage in Tamaulipas; in the Tehuacán Valley maize seeds were being selected for planting and numerous other crops were to be seen in the fields: various species of beans, squash, gourds, the zapotes, and cotton. There is also the possibility that maguey, prickly pear, and mesquite were being planted. In the centuries after 1500 B.C. the Tehuacán Valley peoples became full-time agriculturalists. Approximately fifty percent of their food supply was then obtained from the planted fields.

The agricultural arts were not to be practiced solely in central and northeastern Mexico. Knowledge of farming was to be diffused both north and south. Pod corn was grown in New Mexico in approximately 4000 B.C. Other varieties were also diffused to the American Southwest, and much later to the eastern portions of the continent. Maize was grown in Chiapas in 3000 B.C. and in Peru between 1500 and 1000 B.C. By 500 A.D. most of the Indian peoples of eastern North America were raising fine crops of maize, squash, and beans. In Mesoamerica a maize-squash-bean-chili-amaranth complex had developed. As time passed dry farming techniques were perfected and crops were raised in level and terraced fields as well as in garden plots, increasingly under irrigation.

The agricultural arts brought numerous changes in their wake. The Indian peoples were led first and foremost to a sedentary existence. They were forced to concern themselves with time, the seasons, topography, and water supply. They felt compelled to reorient their religious and ceremonial life. They had to be much more concerned with economic specialization and the division of labor. They had to reorganize politically and socially. Agriculture apparently had helped to produce a major revolution in Indian life. It was a factor of the utmost importance in leading the Olmec, and later the Maya and Aztec, to what we consider "civilization."

LATER DIFFERENTIATION OF THE CULTURES

By the time of the European and later American conquests the Indian cultures of North America had been greatly diversified. Between 1750 and 1800, for example, caribou hunters occupied the Canadian Sub-Arctic, hunters of the new bison moved from place to place on the Great Plains, gatherers of wild seeds occupied the Great Basin, the western plateau, northern Mexico, and much of California, salmon fishermen and hunters of sea mammals lived on the northwest coast, and farmers tilled their precious fields in Mesoamerica, the Antilles, and in the southwest desert. There were peoples in the southeast and northeast who supplemented their agriculture by gathering, hunting, and fishing, and the prairie peoples complemented their garden horticulture by making occasional bison-killing expeditions onto the plains. To complete the picture of the continent in the late 18th and early 19th centuries, a non-Indian people, the Eskimo, were hunting sea mammals on Arctic shores.

THE CULTURE AREAS (C. 1800)

The peoples who lived in these so-called culture areas — the Mandan, the Hopi, the Chipewyan, the Nez Perce, the Comanche, the Aztec, the Yaqui, the Creek — and numerous others, all have their separate tales to tell in time and place. All offer painful, tragic, or sometimes heartening and hopeful examples of the way man lives with respect to his fellow man and the way he perceives and lives in his own environment.

How tragic, for example, the fate of the Mandan — absolute extinction, how heart-rending the plight of the Nez Perce in their struggle to reach Canada and freedom, how crushing the destruction of Aztec Tenochtitlán, and how devastating the annihilation of the Arawak. Yet, how awe-inspiring the creativity of the Haida and Maya, the strength of the Yaqui and Cherokee in the face of constant prodding, the skill of the Seminole in maintaining themselves as a people, the endurance of the Navajo through the "Long Walk" and return to recreating their culture in their old homeland.

There is much indeed to learn about America from the very first Americans. There is much, too, that we must learn about the Indians themselves.

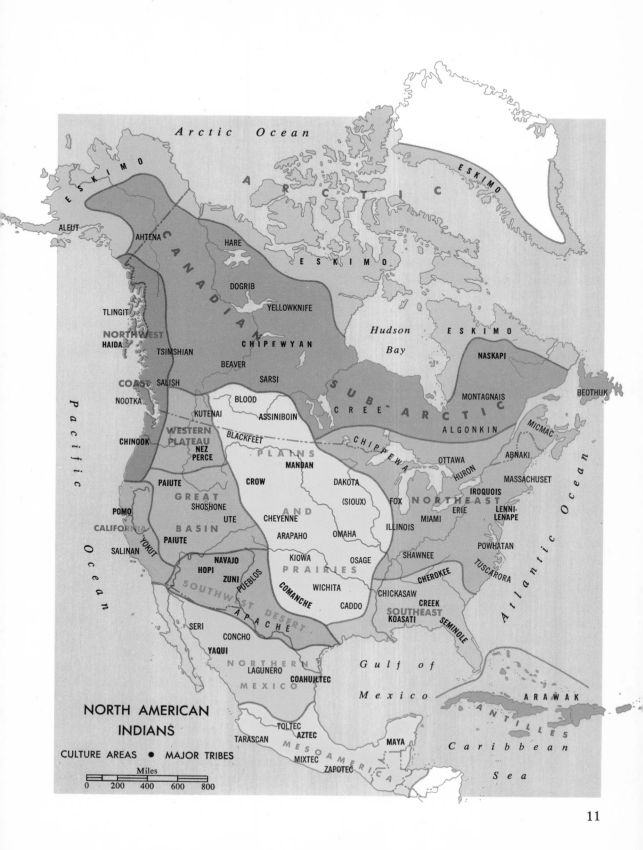

Arctic Ocean

ESKIMO

ESKIMO

ALEUT

AHTENA

HARE

ESKIMO

CANADIAN

DOGRIB

YELLOWKNIFE

Hudson
Bay

ESKIMO

NASKAPI

TLINGIT

NORTHWEST

HAIDA

CHIPEWYAN

TSIMSHIAN

BEAVER

SARSI

MONTAGNAIS

BEOTHUK

COAST

SALISH

NOOTKA

BLOOD

ASSINIBOIN

SUB-ARCTIC

CREE

ALGONKIN

MICMAC

KUTENAI

CHINOOK

WESTERN
PLATEAU

BLACKFEET

CHIPPEWA

ABNAKI

NEZ
PERCE

PLAINS

MANDAN

OTTAWA

HURON

MASSACHUSET

PAIUTE

CROW

GREAT

SHOSHONE

DAKOTA

(SIOUX)

FOX

NORTHEAST

ERIE

IROQUOIS

LENNI-
LENAPE

POMO

UTE

AND

CHEYENNE

MIAMI

CALIFORNIA

BASIN

PAIUTE

ARAPAHO

ILLINOIS

OMAHA

SALINAN

YOKUT

KIOWA

OSAGE

SHAWNEE

POWHATAN

NAVAJO

PRAIRIES

HOPI

ZUNI

PUEBLOS

WICHITA

CHEROKEE

TUSCARORA

SOUTHWEST

COMANCHE

CADDO

CHICKASAW

CREEK

SOUTHEAST

DESERT

APACHE

KOASATI

SEMINOLE

SERI

CONCHO

YAQUI

NORTHERN

LAGUNERO

COAHUILTEC

Gulf of

Mexico

MEXICO

ARAWAK

ANTILLES

NORTH AMERICAN
INDIANS

TOLTEC

AZTEC

TARASCAN

MESOAMERICA

MAYA

Caribbean

CULTURE AREAS ● MAJOR TRIBES

MIXTEC

ZAPOTEC

Sea

Miles

0   200   400   600   800

Pacific   Ocean

Atlantic Ocean

The Southern Tribes

The Southern Tribes inhabited North America from southern Texas to Panama; they also occupied the large island groups of the West Indies. Archaeologists, probing into the area's past, have uncovered a deep time-depth for man's presence there. Man may already have found his way, for example, through Mexico, Central America, and along the northern South American coast by 13,000 B.C. He was most assuredly hunting and trapping animals (now-extinct horses and antelopes, rabbits, gophers, and rats), and collecting a wide variety of plant foods in Mexico's Tehuacán Valley in 10,000 B.C. He was early present in Tamaulipas, lived at Frightful Cave in southern Coahuila in 6900 B.C., and in the Big Bend country of western Texas in 5000 B.C. For millennia apparently man had earned his livelihood by hunting and gathering; he had been a member of a small band, a nomad who wandered from place to place with the seasons. But some time after 7000 B.C. in Tamaulipas and in the Tehuacán Valley he discovered that if he planted seeds in the earth many would sprout, rise, and thrive. In the millennia that followed numerous peoples adopted agriculture and its varying techniques as their own. They planted squash, maize, beans, and other crops. The idea spread in all directions. It found its way to Guatemala, Panama, the northern South American coast, and over the water to the West Indies. It was carried by Indians to the American Southwest and to the American East.

Agriculture was one of the true harbingers of a developing civilization. It encouraged man to organize for a sedentary existence; it taught him the necessity of preoccupying himself with time and its problems; it helped to reorient his views on economic specialization and the division of labor; it stimulated a reexamination of his religion and inspired him to new creativity in the arts; it was in large measure responsible for his ability to sustain a growing population. The first American civilization may well have been produced by the Olmec at La Venta (800-400 B.C.). There in the Tabasco lowlands the first ceremonial centers in what later would be called *Mesoamerica* were created. There the Olmec built fine temples and the Great Pyramid. There they fashioned a significant art style with the were-jaguar as the central theme. There they worked in jade and basalt. At Tres Zapates the Olmec produced hieroglyphs and the "long count" calendar. The Olmec had laid the foundations for civilization in Mesoamerica.

Some scholars suggest that civilization as such can only be traced back to Teotihuacán (c. 300 B.C. — 600 A.D.) or Olmec-derived Monte Alban and the beginnings of true urbanization in the Americas. But be that as it may the illustrious Maya development at least stems directly from the Olmec past.

MESOAMERICA

The Maya reached their apogee during the so-called "Classic" period (300 A.D. - 900 A.D.). In the Petén and in the northern lowland of Yucatán numerous ceremonial centers gleamed in the sun. The causeways and great plaza at Tikal, for example, were lined with countless numbers of people. There was activity in the ball court. Priests performed in the temple-pyramids, architects completed a roofcomb atop the tall temple, artists embellished stelae near the North Acropolis. Trader and warrior, engineer and astronomer, master and slave, carried out their accustomed tasks. And beyond the ceremonial center the *milpas,* or planted fields, yielded rich bounties of maize and possibly yam-like tubers to the hard working farmers. Maya life was apparently rich and full.

But the fall was swift. By the 11th century A.D. the Petén was virtually deserted. No one

lived at Tikal. And the Toltec had already arrived in the northern ceremonial centers. The Maya Classic had come to an end.

The Aztec rise was meteoric; the fall equally swift. As hunters and gatherers they arrived in the Valley of Mexico from the barbarian north in 1248 A.D. Quickly they adopted the ways of their neighbors. In bold steps they proceeded to forge the institutions and strategies that would lead them to empire. A masterful triple alliance, in which they became the dominant partner, was their means to an end. The Aztec would rule by conquest from sea to sea. So successful were they that in their god Huitzilopochtli's name they received tribute in goods and in human sacrificial victims from all the territories over which they held sway. Their *pochteca*, or traders, traveled even further.

The Aztec waxed rich. Tenochtitlán teemed with life. The warehouses bulged. The stomachs were for the most part full. But the Aztec kings, reveling in their wealth, began to isolate themselves further and further from their own people. Montezuma II even called himself god. There were difficulties in the conquered lands. When the Spaniards struck, the neighbors of the Aztec were ripe for rebellion. They rose against their masters. And although the battle for Tenochtitlán was a long one—it lasted for two years (1519-1521) —the Spaniards gained the victory. With time the Aztec were to disappear.

ANTILLES AND NORTHERN MEXICO

When Columbus made his original landfall in the Bahamas the Arawak were, perhaps, on the verge of civilization. They had certainly developed a viable culture. They were village dwellers, agriculturalists, whose fine crops of yuca, maize, beans, and squash — plus the produce from the sea — helped to sustain a population of over 1,000,000 on Hispaniola alone. Society was stratified. There were the

rulers and the ruled, the *caciques,* the commoners, the serfs. There were temples in the plazas. There was trade with the mainland.

But civilization would never evolve among the Arawak. For the Spanish blows were too sharp, too lethal. Work in the mines for extended periods was damaging to Indian health. It tore the social order to shreds. Disease and malnutrition contributed ultimately to Arawak destruction. By 1518 the precious million inhabutants of Hispaniola had dwindled to a mere 11,000. A few short years later the Arawak were no more.

The Yaqui and their Cahitan-speaking neighbors, on the other hand, farther removed from the Spanish evil (northwestern Mexico) persisted. Early Spanish inroads were only made with Yaqui approval. And they harassed their would-be conquerors at every turn. In later years the armies of Sonora and of Mexico swept through the Yaqui towns. The Yaqui retreated but never gave up. Many left their ancestral home for employment in distant places. Some moved into the cities of Sonora and Arizona. Along Río Yaqui population fell from 30,000 in Spanish times to 4,000 in 1886. But by the 1950's the Yaqui had recouped their numbers. There were 10,000 Yaqui on Río Yaqui and hundreds of others in the urban communities of Mexico and Arizona.

The Coahuiltec were marginal peoples. They lived on the periphery of the developing cultures around them. They were peripheral to the American Southwest, to Mesoamerica, to the American East—and even to the plains. They wandered over the countryside in small bands. Their time was spent in securing food. So desperate was their economic situation that when the great ideas of other civilizations passed through their territory the Coahuiltec did not reach out for them. When the Spaniards struck they could only succumb. The Coahuiltec, like the Arawak, are no more.

Maya

Mesoamerica

Maya accomplishments were undoubtedly inspired by the deep human need to create. They were nurtured, however, by contacts with others and by extraordinary successes in agriculture. The earliest farmers in North America probably lived in south central Mexico between 7000 and 5000 B.C. Squash and avocado were certainly planted in the Tehuacán Valley during those years. Maize, amaranth, and a variety of beans, among other crops, were later added to the agricultural assemblage. From the Mexican source-area the knowledge of farming and its techniques probably spread in all directions. Mayan-speaking peoples, moving south into Chiapas and the highlands of Guatemala (2500 B.C.) may well have carried the knowledge with them. By 2000 B.C. small farms, planted in maize, dotted the Guatemalan hillsides. They could even be found in the savanna country of the Petén. The ease of exploiting the natural environment and their skills in agriculture led the Maya to a settled existence. By 1000 B.C. they were already living in numerous densely settled villages. They worked in stone, made fine pottery, built wooden daubed-with-mud houses, and buried their leaders in temples erected on earthen mounds.

In the years that followed the population mounted, and the villages grew larger. They often split into many components, becoming satellites of even larger centers where the gods were worshipped and priests performed their rites and ceremonies. The earliest of these so-called "ceremonial centers" was probably Olmec-built La Venta (800-400 B.C.) in the Tabasco lowlands, well outside the Maya area. But it was undoubtedly from the mysterious Olmec that the Maya learned to build their own ceremonial centers. And with them and their religious inspiration came other significant traits: a magnificent art with the were-jaguar as the central theme, hieroglyphic writing, the famous stelae, and the "long count" calendar, all destined to make notable contributions to the Maya of "Classic" times (300 A.D.—900 A.D.).

The Maya waxed rich. Their *milpas* or planted fields continued to produce bountiful crops. When soils were depleted after several years' use the farmers moved on, cleared new fields, and continued to plant. Only in the Guatemalan highlands did the Maya fall on bad days. Shortly after 400 A.D. conquerors (traders or warriors?) from Teotihuacán in the Valley of Mexico became established in the ceremonial center at Kaminaljuyú. Maya culture there was to have a Mexican flavor. In the hot, wet Petén, however, Maya civilization was approaching its zenith; at Uaxactún, Palenque and Tikal the inner creativity would soon burst into full bloom.

Tikal is, perhaps, an exemplar of Maya creativity—of the Maya Classic. Situated on a hill overlooking the steaming Petén, well-watered and with good farmland nearby, Tikal was a settled location as early as 600 B.C. By 300 B.C. buildings of limestone masonry construction were begun on the site that later-day archaeologists would call the North Acropolis. Through time the acropolis rose in height as stone temples and tombs were set down upon the older buildings. During the Maya Classic, Tikal itself housed as many as 10,000 people, with many more thousands, perhaps, living in the immediate vicinity. Visitors from the countryside might approach the ceremonial center over broad causeways. They might visit in the great plaza flanked by temple-pyramids and the North Acropolis, or might observe the games played in the ball courts. First-time visitors might well have stood in awe before the tallest temple, more than 200 feet high, and they might have gaped in amazement at the palaces in the Central Acropolis, obviously occupied by the Tikal elite. First-time visitors, too, might

have viewed the sculptured stelae and the reliefs that depicted former Tikal rulers. They might have compared the architecture—the corbel vaulting, for example—with that of their own ceremonial centers, or might have paused to read Tikal's glyphic texts.

The ceremonial centers of the Maya Classic were not confined to the Petén. They were also present in the Usumacinta basin (Yaxchilán, Bonampak, and Palenque), north of Tikal (Xpuhil), and in the farthest north and east of the Yucatán peninsula (Uxmal, Labna, and Cobá). Uxmal, for example, set in the low Puuc hills, was a Maya jewel. It was dominated by two temple-pyramids (the Dwarf and the Magician of the Spanish friars), the Governor's House, and the so-called *Monjas* or Nunnery. The latter was itself a palace made up of four distinct buildings arranged in a quadrangle around an interior court. The approach was made from the south side via a flight of stairs and through a gateway surmounted by a corbelled arch. From the court visitors could view the frets and the mask carvings of the rain dragons on the north wall, the serpents, snakes, and statues of men and gods on the other facades, and admire the mosaics depicting the thatched-roof huts of the commoners who lived beyond the confines of the ceremonial center. At Labna stood a temple-pyramid and palace joined by a causeway; at Cobá in northern Quintana Roo temple-pyramids and palaces were built which indicate influences from the Petén. Yet each center was, perhaps, unique albeit all were fashioned from the warp and woof of Classic Maya culture.

The Maya of the Classic had organized a viable society, albeit along class lines. A powerful hereditary elite controlled the land and held political power. Among its members were the nobles, priests, warrior-chiefs, large landholders, and wealthy merchants. The commoners, the great Maya body, were free

Aztec

Mesoamerica

From the Chichimeca, or barbarian lands in the north, numerous peoples have from time immemorial invaded the Valley of Mexico. The rare physical beauty of the land, the unbelievable wealth and opulence of the sophisticated urban communities, the possibilities for lust, rapine, and power, and the challenges of living the "civilized" life long provided both motive and lure for invaders. Why the Aztec moved south, however, is still a mystery. In the 12th century A.D., as inveterate nomads, eaters of wild seeds and grubbers in the earth, they stalked Chichimeca, moving ever southward. In a hillside cave in Michoacán they may well have found the idol whom they called Huitzilopochtli, the Hummingbird. They discovered also that he could speak Nahuatl, their language, and therefore could counsel with them and offer them sage advice. In Michoacán, too, they may have seen Indian tribesmen working the earth, planting maize and other crops, and may have learned from them the agricultural arts. The Aztec, or Mexica as they then called themselves, wandered past Tula, the former Toltec seat of empire, and entered the lake country of the Valley of Mexico (Anahuac) from the northwest about 1215. In 1248 they received permission from the Tepanec of Azcapotzalco to settle at Chapultepec, near the western shore of Lake Texcoco. The Aztec had arrived in the land of their destiny.

Numerous city-states already dotted the world of the five intertwined lakes. Texcoco was dominant in the east, Azcapotzalco lay in the west, Xaltocan controlled the northern approaches to the lake country, and Culhuacán, whose people claimed direct descent from the Toltec, was the prime mover in the south. In the world of the lakes the Aztec became an immediate source of trouble. The Aztec brought down upon themselves their neighbors' wrath by raiding Tenayuca for wives. Culhuacán subdued them and brought many of their number to their own city-state as serfs (1298); others remained on the mainland while a small segment fled to the islands in Lake Texcoco. Those who experienced the Culhuacán captivity, however, learned a great deal. They undoubtedly heard of the white and bearded feathered serpent god, Quetzalcoatl, the god of peace, and his opposition to Tezcatlipoca, the god of war and death. They learned that Quetzalcoatl had journeyed to the Gulf of Mexico, had set sail upon its waters, and had promised to return one day to claim his kingdom. The Toltec tale was indelibly impressed in the Aztec psyche.

The captives learned, too, to build small artificial islands in the shallow waters of the lake. They noted how the Culhuacán and their neighbors accumulated silt from the lake bottom, how they deposited it in large basket-like floats, and anchored the "garden" itself with fast-growing, long-rooted plants. The *chinampa* was the answer to the lack of arable land in the lake world; the Aztec were to use it well. In 1322 the captives of Culhuacán fled to the islands in Lake Texcoco already occupied by their Aztec brethren. Three years later work was begun on the city that was to become the Aztec capital — Tenochtitlán.

Tenochtitlán grew and survived because of the labor of the *macehualtin,* the commoners who built the chinampas, farmed them, and gave battle to all comers. It prospered because of the leadership of an incredible group of nobles, the *pipiltin,* who would ultimately draw up the Aztec design for empire. In the early years, however, Tenochtitlán was dominated by the *calpullis,* or stratified clans. Each calpulli occupied and controlled a section of the capital, maintained its own temples, even fought its own wars. These clans grew powerful but the Aztec, as such, were still largely concentrated on the islands.

In 1375 the decision was made to centralize the administration. The Aztec must have a king — a king from a noble and time-honored line. Acamapichtli, in whose veins the blood of the Toltec was thought to flow, was brought in from Culhuacán. He and his appointed nobles were to sire a new generation of pipiltin who in the future would rule the land.

But the Aztec star was yet to shine. The most formidable power in the lake country in the late 14th and early 15th centuries was Azcapotzalco. That city-state controlled the Aztec water supply at Chapultepec and received Tenochtitlán tribute. The bondage was depressing; the pipiltin must fight to destroy their enemies. Under Itzcoatl the city of Tenochtitlán, in company with Texcoco and Tlacopán, fell upon Azcapotzalco (1429) and thoroughly annihilated it. The victorious allies formed a Triple Alliance which kept the peace in the lake country for ninety years. In the Valley of Mexico it was generally well known that the alliance was dominated by Tenochtitlán—by the power-hungry Aztec.

As Aztec power mounted so did the power of the Aztec gods. Huitzilopochtli, the Hummingbird, the advice-giving god of the migrations, for example, was raised to the Aztec pinnacle. It was he, as decreed by Itzcoatl and his ambitious advisor, Tlacaellel, who would lead the Aztec to their divine destiny; he who would lead the Aztec to empire. The pipiltin would brook no opposition to him. And those who submitted to Aztec power would adopt Huitzilopochtli as their own. They would build a temple in his honor and worship him. When the rulers of Xochimilco refused to provide new building materials for a Huitzilopochtli temple the Aztec overwhelmed them in battle. Hundreds of captives were brought to Tenochtitlán and offered in sacrifice to the Aztec god; their chests were slashed open and their hearts torn from their bodies. As time wore on it became increas-

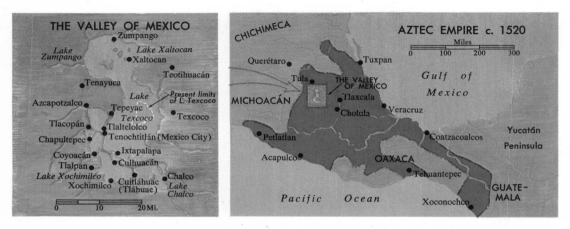

THE VALLEY OF MEXICO

Zumpango
Lake Zumpango
Lake Xaltocan
Xaltocan
Teotihuacán
Tenayuca
Azcapotzalco
Lake Texcoco
Present limits of L. Texcoco
Tepeyac
Texcoco
Tlacopán
Tlaltelolco
Chapultepec
Tenochtitlán (Mexico City)
Coyoacán
Ixtapalapa
Tlalpan
Culhuacán
Lake Xochimilco
Cuitláhuac
Chalco
Xochimilco
(Tláhuac)
Lake Chalco
0   10   20 Mi.

AZTEC EMPIRE c. 1520
Miles
0   100   200   300
CHICHIMECA
Querétaro
Tuxpan
Tula
THE VALLEY OF MEXICO
Gulf of Mexico
MICHOACÁN
Tlaxcala
Cholula
Veracruz
Petlatlan
Coatzacoalcos
Yucatán Peninsula
Acapulco
OAXACA
Tehuantepec
GUATE-MALA
Pacific Ocean
Xoconochco

ingly clear that Huitzilopochtli, and therefore the Aztec, could not survive unless the need for human blood and human hearts was completely satisfied.

The chief weapons of the Aztec warriors were spears tipped with obsidian (volcanic glass) and swords of wood set with jagged obsidian edges. The Aztecs also used bows and arrows, slings and clubs.

Employing Huitzilopochtli as their inspiration the Aztec moved against their near neighbors in the Valley of Mexico and were phenomenally successful. In Huitzilopochtli's name the Aztecs demanded and received specific tribute in goods and a precise levy of sacrificial victims. Fired up by their successes they pushed east toward the hot and low gulf coast and to the far south and west. The long arms of Aztec terror were ultimately to extend from the Valley of Mexico to both coasts and south to Guatemala. The trading arms were to reach even farther, to Nicaragua, Panama, and to distant Colombia.

Trade lay in the hands of the *pochteca* or merchant class. The pochteca may well have served initially as gatherers of intelligence, and may have preceded the warriors into the city-states or communities destined for conquest. As traders they could well supply the Aztec leadership with pertinent information: popula-

tion figures, lists of goods available for tribute, the numbers that could be spared for sacrifice, the names of sympathetic leaders, the unsympathetic, and so on. But as the area over which the Aztec sun shone grew ever larger, the pochteca sought for themselves the role of true merchants. They arranged for the movement of goods, on human backs, to and from the far reaches of the empire. They shipped cloth, rope, and obsidian tools from Tenochtitlán to the hot country. In exchange they received cotton, cacao, rubber, brilliantly colored bird feathers, and gold. Emeralds arrived in Tenochtitlán from the single-source area in Colombia. Pochteca influence provided that warriors accompany the human trade trains. At selected stations warrior garrisons were maintained. The pochteca, of course, grew rich and prosperous. They were able to create their own guild, worship their own god, stay above the law, and live in a segregated section of the capital. They had waxed rich through Aztec conquest, tribute, and trade and, they would hasten to add, through the might of Huitzilopochtli. For the pipiltin and for Tenochtitlán, of course, the very same would be true.

Tenochtitlán had certainly become the queen city-state of the Valley of Mexico. Its heart was the great temple plaza in which stood the twin-stepped, twin-templed pyramid dedicated to Huitzilopochtli, and to Tlaloc, the god of rain and plenty. Nearby were the ball court, the skull-rack, and numerous smaller pyramids. West and south of the great pyramid were the palaces of the Aztec kings. Beyond them in all directions, and often built on canals, were the stone and sun-dried brick homes of the pipiltin and the wattle-and-daub dwellings of the commoners, serfs, and slaves. There were some 60,000 buildings in all, with an estimated population of perhaps 250,000. Water for the city-state was carried by pipe from Chapultepec. Three causeways (they served as dikes as well as avenues), skillfully engineered, carried traffic from the main plaza to the mainland and beyond. One went south to Itzapalapa, another west to Tlacopán, the third past the plaza at Tlaltelolco to Tepeyac. Crowded with people and goods the causeways throbbed with life. So did the canal thoroughfares, the plazas, the temples. And the tribute from the "provinces" continued to arrive. The warehouses literally bulged with material goods. Huitzilopochtli was claiming his exhorbitant levy of human hearts. Tenochtitlán had in the opening decades of the 16th century reached its apogee. So, too, had the Aztec kings.

Itzcoatl, Montezuma I, Axayacatl, Tizoc, and Ahuitzotl, the Aztec kings, had all made significant contributions in raising the Aztec to the heights. But the greatest glory and the complete demise were to be shared by one alone, the self-deified priest-king Montezuma (or Moctezuma) II (1503-1520). Montezuma pressed his power to its limits. He virtually decreed that he, like Huitzilopochtli, was a god. When he passed his people in procession they must immediately press their faces into the earth. Even the pipiltin were forbidden to gaze into his face. Montezuma was god and king. He wanted the world to know that. He appointed only ranking noblemen to office,

sent only the children of pipiltin to schools of higher learning, and dared to replace servants in the most menial tasks with high ranking pipiltin. He kept tight control on the provinces and waged war when he saw fit. Thousands of captives were led to the sacrificial stones.

Montezuma had helped to create, therefore, the conditions for eventual disaster. Noblemen and commoners, cogs in the strict Aztec system, had been driven far apart. A series of poor crop years further alienated the macehualtin. These were the free commoners, by far the largest group within the population, who formed a part of the lower strata of the calpulli. Neighboring city-states were growing restless under repression. There was open rebellion. And in his palace Montezuma began to hear reports of alien visitors who had arrived by sea along the gulf coast. In the lowland communities it was whispered that Quetzalcoatl had returned as promised to reclaim his kingdom. Montezuma was on the verge of panic. But he did not stir.

The Quetzalcoatl of Montezuma's mind was in reality the Spaniard, Hernando Cortés, who with his mounted soldiers arrived on the gulf coast in the spring of 1519. Urged by the pipiltin to fight the fair-skinned newcomers, Montezuma refused. How could he give battle to the legendary Quetzalcoatl? On November 8, 1519, the Spaniards entered Tenochtitlán. But the confrontation proved to be only the beginning. Aztec hostility was aroused when the idol of Huitzilopochtli was dragged from the great temple. They rose in open rebellion, drove the Spaniards from the city, and for his treachery stoned and stabbed Montezuma to death. It was not until August 13, 1521, that the Spaniards could claim conquest of Tenochtitlán. The mighty Aztec had fallen. But today, four and one-half centuries after the conquest, the Aztec countenance can still be seen in the face of Mexico.

Arawak

Antilles

Man has been in the Caribbean area for perhaps 15,000 years. He early occupied big-game hunting sites (mastodon, horse, and ground sloth) on the Río Pedernales in eastern Venezuela. After the extinction of the big animals during the Pleistocene or the Ice Age, many of the inhabitants turned to fishing or the gathering of vegetable foods for their subsistence. Forty-five hundred years ago voyages were being made in dugout canoes from the South American mainland to the islands nearby. Five hundred years later sea voyagers even found their way, perhaps blown far off course, to the Greater Antilles. In the interior of the Orinoco Valley, meanwhile, the vegetable gatherers had become part-time farmers. Between 4,000 and 1,500 years ago they were already cultivating *yuca,* from which cassava cakes were derived, as their major crop. They made fine pottery and introduced both the horticultural and ceramic arts to the occupants of the Venezuelan coast. At the time of Christ, from a base in the quiet waters of the gulfs

of Paria and Cariaco, sleek canoes aided by northward flowing currents sent Indian peoples to occupy the West Indies: the Lesser Antilles and ultimately Puerto Rico, Hispaniola, Cuba, Jamaica, and the Bahamas.

When Columbus made his landfall in the Bahamas (San Salvador, October 12, 1492) he found the islands occupied by the Arawak. Subsequent Spanish voyages disclosed that the Arawak dominated the Greater Antilles as well. Earlier arrivals—they were far more primitive—had been pushed into westernmost Cuba and into the geographical extremities of Hispaniola. It is from the writings of the Spanish chroniclers (Martyr, Oviedo, Las Casas, Pané) that we have obtained our knowledge of the Arawak.

Arawak society, the chroniclers say, was stratified. The *caciques,* or hereditary rulers by matrilineal descent, held sway over large blocks of territory. They were often carried about in litters. Las Casas believed that the cacique of Xaragua was the most important leader in all of Hispaniola. He was a much respected individual; his people were the most polished in manners and speech, and he was served by a distinguished array of nobles. There were also caciques of secondary rank who were leaders in the smaller districts. Both sets of caciques were served by a nobility, a large class of commoners, and a group who were lifelong serfs.

The Arawak lived in numerous villages. Many of these contained 1,000 to 2,000 inhabitants, each comprising twenty to fifty circular, bell-shaped, thatch-roofed houses. The villages were organized around a rectangular plaza, on which the leading cacique's house— larger than the others—fronted. Temples to the *zemi,* the Arawak oracles depicted both in human and animal form, were set up at the ends of the plaza. There the wise old men or shamans recounted the traditions of their people, told the exploits of their great

Greater

San Salvador

Atlantic

Mexico

Cuba

Antilles

Ocean

Santa María
de la Vera Paz

Cibao

Puerto
Rico

ARAWAK

Jamaica

Hispaniola

Caribbean

Sea

Lesser Antilles

G. of
Cariaco

Gulf of
Paria

Venezuela

Río Pedernales

Orinoco R.

men, and preached what they knew of the heavens. The plaza was a public meeting ground, where the caciques held their assemblies and festivals. There the people danced and sang, and amid the gathering throngs the ball games (a Mexican import) were played.

Beyond the villages, spread out for miles, were the farm plots. Many were in the lush green valleys near the coasts, some were along the riverbanks, and others were tucked away between the high mountain frames. For the most part the soil and the more than adequate rainfall helped to provide fine crops. The Arawak did not have to move from place to place. They grew root crops in earthen mounds often heaped knee-high. These mound clusters or tracts, called *canucos,* protected the land against soil erosion and sheet wash. Bitter yuca was the islands' staple; the sweet potato was the second most important crop. But the Arawak also planted maize, beans, and squash and raised peanuts, arrowroot, and tobacco, as well as *bixa,* a shrub from which red body-paint was extracted. In dry Xaragua and Jamaica fine cotton was grown under irrigation.

Because the canucos produced so well and the streams, lakes, and nearby sea provided shellfish, waterfowl and turtles in abundance, population in the trade-wind swept islands literally boomed. In Columbus' day Hispaniola alone could count more than 1,000,000 Arawak heads. There were perhaps a fewer number in Puerto Rico, Jamaica and Cuba. The Arawak had produced a viable culture in a lush environment. The Spaniards could bring them only ruin.

The Spaniards meant to drain the Antilles. They would, using Arawak labor, gather the gold nuggets from the river placers in the Cibao lowland of Hispaniola, and in other places where the precious metal could be found. Columbus himself asked that each and every Arawak pay his tribute. The collections would be made through the caciques who were controlled by their Spanish overlords. Governor Nicolas de Ovando (1502-1509) was even more sanguine. He dominated the caciques completely, thereby crushing the Arawak social organization. He allocated all the natives to the Spanish *encomendero* or to the crown. He organized the hated *demora,* whereby the Arawak were compelled to work six to eight months in the mines, only after which were they returned to their canucos to farm. Later no limits were placed on the number of months any Indian could be required to work.

Meanwhile, Ovando, following instructions from his government, had planted fifteen Spanish towns or villas over the length and breadth of Hispaniola. One such was Santa María de la Vera Paz, which replaced the destroyed Xaragua. The segregated towns were all placed near important Indian population centers. The Spanish *vecinos* waxed rich; the Arawak were nearing their demise.

Work in the mines, moving from one locale to another, the struggles with the Spaniards, the new diseases to which they were not immune, the breakdown of the social order, and an all-pervading malnutrition contributed to Arawak decline. When Ovando's successor, Diego Columbus, counted the heads of Arawak available for work in 1509 he could muster only 60,000. In 1514 there were just over 22,000 on government rolls, and in 1518 only 11,000. The will to live and to reproduce was gone. Occasional Arawak remnants survived in far-off mountain retreats, but for all practicable purposes the Arawak had ceased to be.

Yaqui

Northern Mexico

The Río Yaqui breaks from its gorge in the Sierra Madre Occidental and flows across the lowland to the south and west for more than sixty miles before entering the Gulf of California. Its flow is especially marked during the spring thaw and again in summer when the clouds burst over northwestern Mexico. In the 16th and 17th centuries the river's overflow and the fine alluvium on both riverbanks provided the Cahitan-speaking Yaqui with an excellent environment for growing maize, squash, cotton and beans. The river provided, too, a fine potable water supply. Mesquite and cacti stands thrived away from the river and the earth yielded a wide variety of seeds, roots and wild fruits. Deer were ample in the neighboring mountains and fish and shellfish abundant in and along the Gulf coast. So rich, in fact, was the food resource base that the Yaqui could apparently support a well-fed population of some 30,000.

The Yaqui lived in what the Spaniards would later describe as *rancherías,* or semi-permanent, unpatterned settlements. A typical ranchería of, perhaps, three hundred people might consist of as many as fifty dwellings all of which were either dome-shaped and mat-covered, or rectangular in form with flat roofs and walls of woven cane, or wattle-and-daub. A *ramada,* used for outside cooking, religious ceremonials, and summer sleeping, undoubtedly served a number of dwellings. In the 17th century the Spaniards counted eighty rancherías on both sides of the Río Yaqui. In 1609-1610 a Spanish force under Captain Hurdaide was soundly thrashed by the Yaqui, who were able to muster 6,000 fighting men for the fray, a truly remarkable feat. For the Yaqui had no real tribal consciousness. Each ranchería was virtually an autonomous unit. But the Spaniards were to learn to their sorrow that invaders were harshly treated and that the Yaqui could rise as one against a real enemy.

In the aftermath of Hurdaide's defeat the Yaqui invited, on their terms, Jesuit missionaries to the Yaqui country (1617). Until the time of their expulsion one hundred and fifty years later (1767) the Jesuits were to have a profound and remarkable effect upon Yaqui culture. Although few in numbers the missionaries set themselves immediately to the task. By 1619 they had baptized virtually the entire Yaqui population. By 1623 they had reduced the eighty rancherías to eight Spanish-type pueblos replete with plaza, adobe church, mission house, and beyond these the fenced fields and corrals. Over the years the Jesuits introduced numerous innova-

tions. They brought new crops (including wheat), implements, and techniques to the Yaqui fields; they introduced domestic animals, the art of writing, the six-day work week and a vast number of religious ceremonials. They filled Yaqui minds with concepts of the Cross, the Virgin Mary, the Lord Jesus, and the Trinity, and they introduced the Spanish language to the Yaqui. It is to the credit of the Jesuits that the Yaqui accepted much of what they were offered, albeit with alterations that conformed to Yaqui notions.

Even before the Jesuit expulsion, however, the Yaqui had risen in rebellion (1740). Prime targets were the Spanish civil government and its ever-growing military arm; the Jesuits, longtime friends of the Yaqui, were not to be harmed. At the Hill of Bones, in a disastrous defeat, the Yaqui and their Mayo allies (another Cahitan-speaking tribe) were to loose 5,000 fighting men. The blow was a staggering one. But the Yaqui spirit did not die. Eight decades later, under the dreamer, Juan Banderas, the Yaqui rose once more and in company of Pima, Opato and Mayo kinsmen struck at the newly-formed Sonoran government. Once again the blows were hammer-strong. Banderas' army was badly beaten (1833), its leader executed, and the dream, an independent Indian state in northwestern Mexico, was buried with him.

Meanwhile the Jesuits had long since gone, and the Yaqui communities, in the Yaqui view (certainly not shared by Sonoran and Mexican officialdom), had become autonomous once more. The Yaqui considered themselves free to make their own decisions. They reorganized the government of the Eight Towns, reformed their religious practices, placed new emphasis upon their ceremonials (including the so-called pascola arts in which the *pascola* or entertainers delighted the crowds with dancing, singing, and the recitation of Yaqui history), and completely restructured their military establishment. A well-trained cavalry and infantry equipped with guns and swords would now meet potential invaders. But the burden was much too great. Sonoran and Mexican forces both harassed the Yaqui towns. Yaqui men were forced to abandon the fields. Yields declined conspicuously. Many Yaqui began to leave the river towns for employment in distant mines, haciendas, or fishing villages; some moved to Hermosillo and to other urban communities. By the 1870's the population along the Río Yaqui had been reduced to 9,000. After Cajeme's abortive revolt of 1885-1886, there remained a mere 4,000.

No longer were the Yaqui in control of the ancestral homeland. Mexican settlers surveyed and occupied the land and built a canal network on both sides of the Río Yaqui. And the Yaqui continued to leave the river towns. They moved to far-flung places in Mexico and north into Arizona. Unable to live among the Pima and Papago, whom they considered inferior, the Yaqui established their own *barrios* on the edges of urban communities like Phoenix and Tucson. At home the Yaqui continued to fight. They fought through the Mexican Revolution of 1910 and thereafter until 1918, when peace finally came to the Yaqui country. But it was not until the 1930's that the Yaqui returned to the river in large numbers. In 1939 the Mexican government set aside the north bank and the neighboring mountains for exclusive Yaqui use. By the 1950's there were 10,000 Yaqui in five new towns north of the river. There were Yaqui scattered through Sonora and the American Southwest. By the 1960's the Arizona Yaqui had become much acculturated to the dominant American society while the Sonora Yaqui were succumbing to the dominant Mexican society. Today on both sides of the international boundary the identifiable and indomitable Yaqui live on.

25

Coahuiltec

Northern Mexico

Spanish conquistadores, missionaries, soldiers and settlers, moving north from Mexico City, Guadalajara and Zacatecas in the middle of the 16th century, were struck by the increasing aridity of the landscape. In Coahuila, Nuevo León, and adjacent Texas, the rolling earth was covered with thorny desert plants, shrubs and stunted trees. Various species of agave, cacti and mesquite were ever-present. Much of the land was virtually parched. Many streams were intermittent. When the rains came they came in sudden downpours at infrequent intervals. It was a land, in the Spanish view, in which life could barely survive. Only in the far north, in the shadow of the Balcones Escarpment, did the Europeans find a significant fauna—bison, deer, antelope and collared peccary. For the most part, however, animal life consisted merely of small rodents, particularly rabbits, and reptiles. And, of course, man—the Coahuiltec—who had lived on both sides of the Rio Grande, perhaps for centuries.

Archaeologists, working at Frightful Cave, have established man's presence in southern Coahuila, Mexico, as early as 6900 B.C. Man is also known to have been an inhabitant of the Great Bend country of western Texas in 5000 B.C. In both locales he was a hunter and gatherer. He knew the use of spear and dart, employed the *atlatl* (spear thrower), and pounded seeds with wooden pestles. His lifeway apparently remained little changed for centuries. The advent of agriculture in neighboring Tamaulipas and in distant Puebla, for example, was undoubtedly known to the early inhabitants of Nuevo León and Coahuila, but cultivation of crops was never adopted. Climatic conditions, perhaps, made acceptance impossible. But the knowledge of farming did spread through northeastern Mexico into Texas and beyond. Between the 12th and 14th centuries A.D., however, man in southern Coahuila was still a small-game hunter who used the bow and arrow; he was probably also still a gatherer of wild seeds. When Cabeza de Vaca, the intrepid Spanish explorer, was cast ashore on the Texas coast in 1528 (he later traveled inland), he found the Coahuiltec hunting the rabbit and small rodents, and collecting the fibers, leaves, and bulbs of the agave, as well as mesquite pods.

The Coahuiltec of historic times were not a tribe as such, but rather a collection of numerous bands or family groups (over 200) organized patrilineally, who wandered over the countryside from Chihuahua to Tamaulipas and north into Texas. Completely autonomous, the bands were led by the most able hunters and warriors among them. Sustenance was the chief concern. For most of the year individual bands were kept busy scouring the niggardly earth for a food supply. Only in summer did several combine to engage in communal hunting. Small animals were snared or trapped. Rabbits were surrounded, forced into a smaller-growing circle, and clubbed to death. Deer, where available, were brought to earth by bow and arrow. On the few water bodies fish were lured by torch, killed by arrow, or taken in nets. But the prime source of food in the Coahuiltec country were the plants. Bulbs of agave were gathered, roasted in pits, ground into flour, and either eaten or stored. From agave leaves, *mescal,* a stimulating drink, was produced. *Peyote,* cactus derived, was made into a tea. The fruit of the prickly pear was carefully picked. Mesquite pods were lifted from the trees. The sweet beans within were eaten, while excess amounts were pounded into flour and stored. Mesquite flour, mixed with various seeds and berries, was the concoction that the Spaniards would call *mesquitamal.* The Coahuiltec search for food was never-ending. In lean years they scoured the countryside for lizards, snakes, worms, and spiders. They consumed ant eggs, deer dung, and earth.

Competition for hunting and gathering grounds and for women often led to band warfare. It was often the women who goaded their men into the struggles. Challenges were issued and numerous hit-and-run battles fought. Victorious warriors would return for scalp dances. The scalps themselves were hung conspicuously on short poles set in a line. The warriors danced around the poles. Then the women, their faces smeared with charcoal, removed the scalps and danced around the poles themselves. Unfortunate captives were roasted and often eaten.

Coahuiltec life was most difficult at best. It was a life rigorously controlled by demons and spirits—creatures that must be assuaged. It was a life often lived on the periphery of starvation, of constant struggle. It was a life in which there was little socialization. It was a life, nevertheless, in which the Coahuiltec had to give thanks for each year's blessings. Therefore, the *mitote,* or the all night dance and feast, was held during the hot summer. Several bands often joined together for the festivities. Participants, both men and women, dressed in their best, took peyote, and to the music of drum and rattle danced far into the night. Many fell into a trance. During the early morning hours a shaman might address the assemblage. Eating was constant. The music did not stop. By daybreak, however, the mitote had come to its end. But the Coahuiltec world was already a better place in which to live.

In the 17th century the Coahuiltec country was traversed many times by Spanish expeditions. In 1677 a Franciscan mission was established at Nadadores, and before the end of the century others were established in the Rio Grande drainage and near San Antonio. By 1776, when Jacobo Ugarte y Loyola was completing his final year as Governor of Coahuila, the Spaniards were firmly entrenched in northeastern Mexico. Numerous pueblos,

villas, and presidios dotted the landscape. Apache marauders from the north, however, continued to make raids upon the settlements directly across the Rio Grande and on the western flank of Coahuila through the Bolsón de Mapimí. For the Coahuiltec the end had virtually arrived. Smallpox and mission life had reduced their numbers sharply, and raids by Apache and Comanche had taken the flower of their manhood. By the beginning of the 19th century the Coahuiltec of Texas had disappeared, and by the end of the century the Coahuiltec of northeastern Mexico had also vanished.

The Eastern Tribes

The haunts of the Eastern Tribes were in the great land area between the Northern Forest and the Gulf of Mexico, and between the Mississippi River and the eastern ocean. Some of the tribes spent their lives near the sea, others near the lakes and rivers of the deep interior. There were Indians on the Coastal Plain and in the mountains and valleys of the Appalachian system. There were Indians near the Great Lakes and in the Mississippi River Valley.

The Eastern Tribes shared many common cultural features. They were devoted to farming as their chief means of subsistence. They supplemented their agricultural pursuits by hunting, gathering, and fishing. The men were the hunters and most often the fishermen. Women were the farmers and were held in high regard. They often made important decisions in clan and moiety. The Eastern Tribes were politically sophisticated. A number of them banded together and formed confederations to solve mutual problems. Eastern tribesmen were exceptionally able warriors. They carried the arrow and warclub across the face of eastern America.

The Eastern Tribes showed remarkable resistance in the face of the European onslaught. Many of the tribes were quick to adapt to changing times; there were those, however, who changed only reluctantly. The fact that a number of the tribes still retain their reservation lands in or near their original locations is a matter of great interest, but the fact that many of the Eastern Tribes were forced to migrate to lands west of the Mississippi is indicative of the savage force thrust upon them.

NORTHEAST

The Iroquoian-speaking tribes, for example, occupied the far north — the area between Georgian Bay and the Susquehanna River. They knew the four seasons including winter's deep chill. They milked the sugar maple, made their canoes and houses of bark, and often fortified their villages with moat and palisade. They were indomitable hunters and warriors who carried tomahawk and warclub, and spread havoc between the St. Lawrence and Ohio rivers. The Six Nations — the Seneca, Cayuga, Onondaga, Oneida, Mohawk and Tuscarora — knew the "Three Sisters" (maize, squash and beans) and reveled in their charms. Iroquois women were fine agriculturalists. They held an important place in the Iroquois social order. They dominated the *ohwachira,* the extended family, had strong voices in the clans and moieties, and when the tribes formed their League, or Longhouse, in the 16th century they exerted their influence in the election of sachems. The formation of the League was one of the crowning Iroquois glories. It brought together the warring Iroquois tribes and it forged an instrument that was to help determine the ultimate fate of North America.

While the Iroquois were early influenced by the French and Dutch, it was English persistence in the person of William Johnson, who helped bind the Iroquois to the English cause. Iroquois warriors fought beside the English in the French and Indian Wars and many remained loyal to them during the Revolutionary War and the War of 1812. As a result of the Revolution, however, the Iroquois League foundered because the individual tribes could not come to a unanimous decision. But while the League itself died, the Iroquois themselves remained strong. To this day they still occupy portions of the ground on which white men knew them in the 17th and 18th centuries.

Farther south in eastern Pennsylvania, southeastern New York, all of New Jersey and neighboring Delaware lived numerous Indian peoples who in aboriginal times carried on separate existences. The notion of

the tribe did not exist. It was only in the face of the coming of the Europeans — the Dutch, Swedes and English—that the distant villages confederated. They became known far and wide as the Lenni-Lenape, the "real," or "original people," as they called themselves or the *Delaware* as the English termed them.

Confederation did not make a single unit of the Lenni-Lenape. The Europeans recognized at least three Lenni-Lenape divisions. The Munsi (or Munsee) in the north, the Unami in the central portions, and the Unalachtigo in the south. The Munsi, neighbors of the Iroquois, fortified many of their villages; the Unami and Unalachtigo did not.

Like the Iroquois the Lenni-Lenape were farmers. The women cared for the crops and gathered berries, fruits, and roots in the forest. The men were the hunters and fishermen. Unfortunately for the Lenni-Lenape since their numbers were few (less than 10,000) they could not withstand the European onslaught. Munsi tribesmen began to leave the Delaware River villages as early as 1690. And despite valiant efforts on the part of the missionaries the Lenni-Lenape could not prevail in their original homeland. By 1802 they had been completely expelled from their New Jersey lands.

SOUTHEAST

In the deep south, in the warm balmy country, lived numerous tribes, the best known of which were the Cherokee, Creek, Seminole, Chickasaw, and Choctaw — later to be called the Five Civilized Tribes. They, too, engaged in agriculture with the women as the farmers. Here too the female was held in high esteem. The men were the hunters and warriors. The Creek, like the Iroquois, lived in settled communities, in towns and villages along the river valleys of Alabama and Georgia. Their towns featured the public square, the hot house and chunkey yard. Be-

yond the square were the individual rectangular frame houses and the clan-owned fields. At mid-18th century there were some 20,000 Creeks living in as many as 50 towns on the Chattahoochee, Flint, Coosa and Tallapoosa.

The Creeks, too, could boast of a league, or a confederacy. Representatives from all of the Creek towns met once each year — a favorite place was Tukabatchee — to discuss problems of mutual concern, to argue the events of waging war or maintaining peace, and to plan for the future.

First meetings with the Europeans were quite peaceful. The French and English traders brought much-wanted goods to the Creek towns. Deer, otter and beaver pelts were exchanged for guns, metal goods and English *stroud* cloth. Creek women began to sport English and French calicos. Guns gradually replaced the use of bows and arrows. The clan system began to break down as more and more marriages were made between Indian and European.

But nothing was so devastating to the Indian as the European—and later American — drive for land. Settlers in Georgia and Alabama made forays upon the Indians. The Indians retaliated. After prolonged struggles the Indian resistance was broken. The Creeks were forced to leave their homeland. Between 1836 and 1840 they moved to Indian Territory. The migration of the Cherokee was equally disheartening. They were forced to walk what has been described as the "Trail of Tears." But they did leave a remnant of their people in the hills of North Carolina that later was to flourish. The Seminoles too experienced much difficulty. They were harried by the Georgians and Carolinians. They moved deeper into Florida where they were harassed by the military. Finally the large majority were moved to Oklahoma although a remnant, a well known one, still lives near the Florida Everglades.

Iroquois

Northeast

In the 15th and early 16th centuries the Iroquois country was bathed in blood. Intermittent warfare was waged by Iroquoian-speaking peoples upon each other in the area between Georgian Bay and the Susquehanna River. Particularly aggravating was the chronic fighting and bloodletting in the heart of the Iroquois territory — the Finger Lakes area of central New York, and the Genesee and Mohawk River valleys. There the Cayuga, Onondaga and Oneida, the Seneca and Mohawk made war upon each other and their neighbors. So great was the slaughter, so frightening the loss of life that voices calling for moderation, restraint, and even for peace began to be heard from the Hudson to the distant Genesee.

Oral tradition suggests that one of the voices calling for peace was the voice of *Deganawidah*. Deganawidah, the voice of all the Iroquois, pleaded for a cessation of hostilities, for the forging of a Great Peace, and for a confederation of the tribes then vowing each others' destruction. Hiawatha, a Mohawk sachem, took up Deganawidah's call. He visited all the tribes, pleading as Deganawidah had for the Great Peace. The Mohawk, Oneida, Seneca, and Cayuga heeded Hiawatha's words. Only Atotarho, the great sachem of the Onondaga, held out. He would only agree to the Great Peace, to the confederation, if the Onondaga were recognized as leaders, that they would be represented in the confederation by fourteen of the fifty sachems, that they would chair all discussions, and that the meetings of the confederation would be held in Onondaga territory. Hiawatha, reluctantly perhaps but full of hope, agreed to the terms. Sometime, therefore, in the 16th century the League of the Iroquois— the *longhouse* — was born. And peace came to the Iroquois lands.

The Iroquois, about 7,000 strong, lived in small villages near the lakes or rivers. Moats and wooden palisades often protected the village inhabitants. Onondaga, one of the larger villages and capital of the League, was unfortified. Within its confines were 140 bark-covered longhouses, and beyond them the fields tended by the Onondaga women. Maize, squash and beans — the *Three Sisters* of the Iroquois — were planted in the same field. Separate fields were devoted to melons, tobacco and sunflowers. While the Iroquois placed great reliance upon the Three Sisters for subsistence, they also hunted a wide variety of animals, including the deer and bear. They also caught fish, gathered numerous plant foods, and produced countless vats of maple syrup and sugar.

Family life centered around the *ohwachira*, or extended family, at the head of which a woman served. Since residence was matrilocal, newly married daughters brought their husbands to their own mother's longhouse to live. Women therefore tended to dominate the ohwachira. They were also prime decision-makers in the Iroquois clans (the Mohawk and Oneida had Deer, Turtle, and Wolf clans, and the Onondaga many others) and moieties. Their decisions influenced markedly the election of sachems to the League council. The Iroquois have often been cited as an excellent example of a near-matriarchate, but the view is being challenged today by Iroquois scholars.

While the ohwachira flourished and the Three Sisters turned smiling faces upon the Iroquois a great rumble was heard in the north. Mohawk men ceased to make their elm-bark canoes, their tomahawks and pipes. Their children ceased to play their summer games. The medicine men of the False Face Society ceased carving the new False Faces on the basswood trees. For the French under Samuel de Champlain had arrived in the Iroquois country (July 30, 1609). Two Mohawk sachems were killed in the battle that followed, thereby earning for the French the undying hatred of the Mohawk and, through the League, the enmity of all the Iroquois.

The Dutch and the English were far more successful. Dutch firearms, passed from Fort Orange (Albany) to the Mohawk and west to the Seneca made of the Iroquois a formidable military power. English diplomacy and strength, largely in the person of William Johnson, helped to establish a strong Iroquois-English alliance.

William Johnson, fresh from Dublin (1738), settled in the Mohawk country and became a fast and trusted friend of the Indians. He learned their ways and spoke their language with great eloquence. His second wife, Caroline, was the niece of Hendrick, head sachem of the Mohawk; his third wife, Molly Brant, was a full-blooded daughter of the Mohawk Wolf clan. In Mount Johnson (built in 1742) and Johnson Hall (built in 1749) the Johnsons entertained both Indian and white man alike. During the French and Indian War Johnson, who had been appointed Indian Agent by Governor George Clinton, kept the Iroquois on the side of the British.

Later Joseph Brant, Molly's brother, who grew up under Johnson's tutelage, began to exercise his own qualities of leadership. He translated the Gospel of St. Mark and a prayer book into Mohawk. He assisted the missionaries in their work among his own people. In 1775 he visited England and gained enthusiasm for the English in their struggle with the American colonials. Joseph Brant left his beloved Mohawk country for the north and west because of the pressure from American settlers. He settled at Niagara, and in 1779 he secured for the Six Nations (the Tuscarora had joined the Iroquois fifty-seven years earlier) the land on the Bay of Quinte and the lands along Grand River in Ontario.

It was during the Revolutionary War that the grand League of the Iroquois fell apart. The member tribes could not make a unani-

mony, the most important ceremonial of the Lenni-Lenape phratries. The Wolf phratry celebrated for eight days, the Turkey phratry for twelve. They gave thanks for the events of the preceding year, described their visions, danced, and feasted. Clan and phratry *sachems,* or leaders, and shamans collected *wampum* from the participants. Each year the Big House Ceremony brought "peace" to the Lenni-Lenape.

But there was no peace. For the Lenni-Lenape were to come into intimate contact with European traders and settlers. The Dutch, from their Manhattan Island base, crossed the Hudson River in 1618 and established a small trading post called Bergen on the western shore. This was the forerunner of a number of Dutch settlements laid out on the Palisades ridge. Dutch settlements were also attempted in the Raritan and Delaware river valleys. The Dutch exchanged metal tools and knives, beads, liquor and cloth for Lenni-Lenape furs. The Swedes on the Delaware River (1638) had similar experiences. But the Lenni-Lenape country could not supply the furs that the Dutch and Swedes wanted and needed. Finally, the Dutch virtually bypassed the Lenni-Lenape and made trading overtures to the Iroquois, thus straining Lenni-Lenape-Iroquois relations. Both tribes would ultimately take to the warpath.

The loss of much of the fur trade and the struggle with the Iroquois hurt the Lenni-Lenape considerably. Permanent English settlement was to crush them thoroughly. Elizabethtown was founded in 1664. Shrewsbury and Middletown were planted in 1665, Piscataway and Woodbridge in 1666. Robert Treat landed on the shores of the Passaic River in the same year, was warned off the land by the Hackensack, but made the purchase which was to become Newark in 1667. English settlement with its encroachment on Lenni-Lenape territory could not be stopped.

The Lenni-Lenape therefore prepared to move west. Munsi groups are known to have left the Delaware River Valley as early as 1690. Others were soon to follow.

The years after 1700 were particularly bitter for the Indians who stayed in the Lenni-Lenape homeland. They were forced to give up more and more land. They packed their few belongings and moved from one river valley to the next; they succumbed to liquor and disease. And after 1720 the Iroquois, victors in the long wars, became "masters" of the Lenni-Lenape, who were then forced to pay an annual tribute. The Iroquois called the Lenni-Lenape "women." Appeals to clan and phratry, to the sachems and shamans, seemed to help very little. Even the Manito could do nothing for the Lenni-Lenape, who became helpless and thoroughly confused.

It was during this period that the missionaries came to labor among the Indians. David Brainerd, ordained a minister in 1744, preached to the Munsi on the Delaware. In the same year he was at the Unami site near present-day Freehold. He worked very hard but the settlers fought him at every turn. He and his Indian friends were forced to leave. They formed a church, Bethel, at Cranbury. But David Brainerd, afflicted by tuberculosis since early youth, died in 1747, at the age of twenty-nine. Very little had come of his efforts. John Brainerd succeeded his brother at Bethel and like him worked with passionate devotion among his charges. But Bethel failed. The Lenni-Lenape were wracked with disease. Title to their land was taken from them. Brainerd, also ill with tuberculosis, was dismissed by his superiors (1755).

When 3,000 acres of land in Burlington County were purchased for the first Indian reservation in the United States in 1758, John Brainerd was recalled. Two hundred Lenni-Lenape, mostly Unami, were assembled at Edgepelick, or Brotherton. Homes, a store, a sawmill, a school and a meeting house were built. Brainerd stayed with the Indians for ten years. But the Brotherton reservation was not particularly successful. At length, the Lenni-Lenape were invited by Indian friends to lands near New Stockbridge, New York. There the last of the Lenni-Lenape settled and left the state of New Jersey for all time. The year was 1802. The first Indian reservation in the United States had failed.

The great majority of Lenni-Lenape, of course, had already moved west. They lived at times in Pennsylvania, Ohio and Indiana. During their travels they changed considerably. The old culture fell into limbo. Even the Big House Ceremony, the cementing agent of tribal consciousness, was considerably altered. And because they came into contact with numerous enemies in the west they became warriors of great skill. They were feared far and wide. They waged war on the white settlements and on their old Iroquois enemies. In 1789, with permission from the Spanish government, a number of Lenni-Lenape families settled in Missouri and later in Arkansas. By 1820 they were known in Texas. In 1835 more than one thousand Lenni-Lenape were living on a reservation in Kansas. But American settlers moving west continued to harass them. They were finally removed to Indian Territory in Oklahoma in 1867. There they shared the lands of others, chiefly the Cherokee Indians.

In 1924 the Big House Ceremony, albeit different, was still being held. It was even revived briefly during World War II.

The Lenni-Lenape, though all but assimilated, have not completely disappeared. Today nearly two thousand Indians, who call themselves Delaware (or Lenni-Lenape), still live in Oklahoma and north of Lake Erie in Ontario, Canada. Over two hundred and fifty are included in the headcount of the Stockbridge-Munsee in Wisconsin.

Creeks

Southeast

Creek warriors were at home on and near the sun-baked waters of the American Southeast. Their towns and villages (some 50 of them in mid-18th century) lay on the Chattahoochee and Flint, as well as the Coosa and Tallapoosa rivers. Aboriginally their lands had extended from west of the Alabama River to the Atlantic Ocean, but English settlement in Georgia by 1750 had already pressed the Indians westward. When Creek war parties made forays to the Tombigbee River they were in effect encroaching upon Choctaw territory.

The Creeks were not an Indian tribe as such but a conglomeration of various and sundry "tribes." Dominant among these were the Muskogee who spoke the northern Muskhogean tongue. Abihka, Coosa, Coweta, Kasihta, and Tukabatchee, for example, were all Muskogee towns. Tuskegee, Alabama, and Koasati, southern Muskhogean-speaking tribes, had all joined the Creek Confederacy, as had a number of Hitchiti-speaking tribes. The many joiners conformed for the most part, the variations were slight, to the dominant Muskogee or Creek culture. Late in the 18th century the total population stood at about twenty thousand.

Creek towns ranging in population from 200 to perhaps a thousand were all centered about a public square. Four one-story rectangular buildings of wooden frame were set up in a square facing the cardinal points of the compass. Facing east was the building given over to the men of highest rank; the "second men," those who served as advisors to the civil chief or *micco,* occupied the building on the north; on the south side stood the building of the warriors; facing west the edifice containing apparatus for making town repairs or the cabin of the young people. The town square was the public meeting place. There the town leaders met each day to discuss preparations for war, to arrange details

for religious ceremonies, or simply to converse among themselves.

Near the southwest corner of the square the Creeks laid out their summer playground — the *chunkey yard* — where the numerous clans could participate in the ball-play or lacrosse. In the center of the chunkey yard was erected an obelisk of pine, from which was suspended a pennant, a prime target in the bow and arrow contest. In former times short "slave posts" to which war captives were bound and subsequently tortured were also found in the chunkey yard. By 1750 they were no longer in use. At the northwest corner stood the *hot house* or *chokofa,* the Creeks' winter playground. In this circular, windowless, pyramid-shaped and often smoke-filled structure the Creeks played and danced during the winter cold. Beyond the formal public square were the Creek dwellings, those of the rich patterned after the public square itself; those of the poor were single frame houses strewn without pattern through the forest.

Beyond the houses stretched the clan-owned farmland. Fields were planted with maize, squash, pumpkins, beans, and after their introduction by Europeans, melons, potatoes and rice. Planting, tending and harvesting were largely the work of the women. The men were the hunters and fishermen. They hunted deer, bear, beaver, otter, raccoon, and squirrel with black hickory or locust bow, and cane arrows. They were adept in the use of the cane blow gun and the white man's firearms. They fished with hook and line, spear, and hand net and practiced the art of fish poisoning. They stored a fixed portion of their food in a public granary. Thus they protected themselves during war emergencies against poor yields, and permitted travelers through their country to be fed at the expense of the entire community.

By 1750 European traders had become

significant factors in the Creek economy. The English, operating from Charleston and Augusta, and the French from Mobile supplied the Creek towns with guns, powder, razors, needles, knives, woolen goods, blankets, brandy and blue and red cloth in exchange for deer, otter, and beaver skins. *Stroud cloth* from the English and *limbourg* from the French made drastic changes in Creek clothing habits, particularly among the women. They enjoyed wrapping the bright colored calicos around their bodies. French influence waned when by the Treaty of Paris in 1763 the French ceded most of their possessions in North America.

English and later American pressures compelled the Creeks to tighten the reins on the Confederacy. When Alexander McGillivray, half Scotsman, half Creek, became the acknowledged leader of his people he saw to it that the war miccos gained ascendancy over the civil miccos in the representative town bodies. The civil miccos resisted but to no avail. After McGillivray's death on February 17, 1793, no man of sufficient force and tact

appeared to take his place. The structure of town government reverted to its former pattern.

Despite the numerous changes that were taking place all about them and that were visible daily, the Creeks continued their old-time practices. They continued to worship the "Master of Life," and all the living things in the Creek country; they feasted and then fasted during the *busk,* the green corn ceremony, and cleansed themselves by partaking of the Black Drink, a strong emetic; they entered the sweat lodge before making hunting forays into the neighboring forest; they fashioned nets and pots, the cane blowgun, and baskets using the twilled-plaiting technique; they continued to marry outside of their own clans; they cured the sick by reciting the proper chants, applying vegetable potions, and sucking the diseased parts; they buried the dead warrior in a sitting position (in a hole four feet deep under his own house) with warclub, medicine bag, and favorite pipe by his side.

But the Creek world was disintegrating. The enemies now were American innovations

—the tilling of the soil by man, the fencing of the fields, private land ownership — and the Americans themselves, the Georgians and Alabamians, whose numbers were constantly mounting. When Tecumseh went south to rouse the southern tribes against the Americans in 1811, he found only lukewarm support. The Creeks themselves were hopelessly divided. There were those who supported innovations and Americans both and there were those who were violently opposed to anything new, including Americans. In the War of 1812 these rallied to the support of Great Britain. On August 30, 1813, an anti-American force fell upon Ft. Mims on the Alabama River and slaughtered numerous pro-American Indians as well as several hundred settlers. In retaliation General Andrew Jackson, with a force of 3,500 soldiers, annihilated the Creeks who opposed him at Horseshoe Bend, March 27, 1814. In the ensuing treaty the Creeks ceded all of their choice lands in Alabama, as well as a strip of territory on the Georgia-Florida boundary, to the United States.

But the worst was yet to come. Under the Creek Treaty of 1832 the Indians were compelled to cede all of their lands east of the Mississippi. The only exceptions were homestead allotments made to miccos and heads of families. Meanwhile the land-hungry Georgians and Alabamians applied pressure for complete removal. Demoralized and virtually at the point of annihilation several young Creeks took it upon themselves to murder white families. The crimes brought the government order for removal of the Creeks to the Indian Territory. Between 1836 and 1840 columns of Creeks, men, women, and children, at the mercy of Southerners who seized their property and private contractors who supplied their food and transportation, moved ever so slowly to the Indian Territory. It is estimated that half of the Creeks did not survive the

journey west and the early years in the new territory.

The migrants were met at Ft. Gibson by Roley McIntosh and the Creeks of the Verdigris and Arkansas rivers, who had been in the Indian Territory since 1829. Many had prospered. While a number of the new immigrants remained on the Arkansas most settled on the rich earth near the Canadian River. There they rebuilt their lives and old institutions. There they were ministered to by Presbyterians, Methodists and Baptists. There they built their schools and tended their fields. Both contingents, the Arkansas River and the Canadian River Creeks, united politically (1839) to form the Creek Nation. Each retained, however, a principal as well as a second chief as did the individual towns. It was not until 1867 that the Creeks actually united under one government with one set of national officers.

Meanwhile, the Creeks, badly divided, had fought on both sides during the Civil War. By the treaty that followed the conflict the Creeks lost the entire western portion of their tribal domain. With discovery of coal in the Indian Territory, the awarding of grazing contracts, and the coming of the railroad, great pressure was brought by whites to open up the country. On May 2, 1890, the Oklahoma Territory was organized adjacent to the Indian Territory. White population mounted and intruded into Indian lands. The Indians themselves decided to push for Indian statehood. Under the prime influence of Pleasant Porter, the Creek chieftain, they proposed the creation of the State of Sequoyah. But agitation for single statehood was strong. The twin territories were together organized as Oklahoma in 1906, and the new state was admitted to the Union in 1907. The Creek Nation, of course, was accordingly dissolved. Today over 13,000 Creeks still live in northeastern Oklahoma.

Koasati

Southeast

The Koasati, like other members of the Creek Confederacy, were caught up in the epic struggle between the great European powers for control of the North American continent. English and French traders, for example, vied for favored status in the Koasati town. During the decades 1740-1760 the French were clearly in ascendancy. French guns, powder and limbourg (a kind of cloth) could more easily be delivered to the Alabama and Koasati towns from Mobile Bay than similar goods could have been brought inland from English factories on the Atlantic coast. The Koasati *micco,* or leader, could point out, too, that French manufactured goods were infinitely superior to their English counterparts. The French were also militarily active. To seal their hegemony in the Creek country they had built Ft. Toulouse near the Coosa-Tallapoosa confluence.

When the French ceded their possessions in North America in 1763 many Koasati families, longtime friends of the French, began to leave the Koasati town. Some settled on the Tombigbee River, but later returned. In 1795 twenty families moved to the Red River in Louisiana, and then to eastern Texas. During a trip through the Creek country in 1798-1799, Benjamin Hawkins, agent to the Creeks and superintendent of the Southern tribes, could describe the still-thriving mother Koasati town as

"... compact ... situated three miles below the confluence of Cossau and Tallapoosa, on the right bank of Alabama; they have fields on both sides of the river; but their chief dependence is a high, rich island, at the mouth of Cossau. They have some fences, good against cattle only, and some families have small patches fenced, near the town, for potatoes."

But the Koasati continued to leave. In 1822 Jedediah Morse reported 350 Koasati on the Red River. Twenty-eight years later most of

the Red River Koasati had joined kinsmen on the Trinity, Neches, and Sabine rivers in Texas. Still another group chose lands along the Calcasieu River near Kinder, Louisiana. There they promptly laid out their public square, and their settlement became known locally as "Indian Village." When inhabitants of the Koasati towns in Texas were struck by an epidemic they turned to Indian Village for succor. By the time of the Civil War 250 Koasati were living on the Calcasieu.

But there was no rest for the Koasati. Land purchases by whites on the Calcasieu forced the tribesmen to move once more. Persuaded by friends to become landowners themselves, they purchased fine prairie acreages on either side of Bayou Blue, near Elton, Louisiana. The year was 1884.

When Paul Leeds, a Congregationalist minister, arrived on Bayou Blue in 1893 he described them this way:

"Small bark-roofed huts were their homes; game, corn and wild fruits in season their main diet, and drinking liquor, wild dancing and a crude form of racket ball formed their usual pastime. There is no evidence that they were a treacherous or warlike people, or ever participated in a massacre of the whites. Their women were usually chaste and faithful to their husbands and they were generally a peaceful and harmless folk."

Leeds, however, set as one of his missions in life to correct Koasati evils as he understood them. From his pulpit at St. Peter's Congregational Church on Bayou Blue, built especially for the Indians, he preached against the ball-play, against tribal dances, against consumption of alcoholic beverages. Ball-play and dances were carried on in secret for a number of years after Leeds' arrival but were ultimately discontinued.

In the earliest days on Bayou Blue the Koasati relied solely upon hunting, gathering

wells and laid out canal systems and laterals. They watched as the limpid waters rolled over the land. They, and the Midwestern farmers who followed, introduced the binder, reaper, and tractor. They saw rice become the leading commercial crop on the southwestern Louisiana prairie. In 1910 Odell Bertrand, himself a French-speaking rice farmer, purchased land near the Koasati community itself. Before long he was hiring Koasati as field hands. The innovation was of marked significance. The Koasati largely abandoned their traditional subsistence hunting, fishing, and farming, and they became wage laborers instead, remaining so to this very day.

The Koasati, 250 strong, still live on Bayou Blue. The children attend the public schools in Elton. Attendance at St. Peter's Congregational Church is excellent. An occasional mortar and pestle, cane blowgun, bow and arrow, or twilled-plaited or coiled basket can still be found in the community. A micco is still elected. But for the most part the traits dating from the Creek past have not been retained. The same can be said for the small Koasati community in Oklahoma, and for the Alabama-Koasati (Coushatta) reservation near Livingston, Texas. The language, a most conservative trait, and all the Koasati speak it, persists, but it, too, is changing. There is now no Koasati term for tomato or succotash. No distinctions are made today between orange and yellow, or blue and green. The Koasati know the airplane as *pithlaweca,* or flying bird. To make certain that the language is never lost Tulane University anthropologists have systematically recorded it.

For the Koasati themselves, despite their cohesiveness, the Indian memory grows dim. Knowledge of all but the immediate past is virtually nil. There are even those who suggest, for example, that the Koasati have never moved but that the tribe has spent its life on Bayou Blue.

and fishing for their livelihood. They practiced no agriculture. Several years were to pass before small subsistence gardens, carefully tended by the women and children, began to appear behind their dwellings. It is significant that no public square was laid out on Bayou Blue, no *chunkey yard,* no *hot house* (see under Creeks) — all traditional Creek practices. The church, the trails through the piney woods, the graveyard, the at-random location of the dwellings, and later, the disposition of the fields, provided the only distinguishable settlement pattern.

Meanwhile the French rice farmers had arrived in southwestern Louisiana. They dug

Cherokee

Southeast

Cherokee origins have been traced to the Canadian north, the Great Lakes area, and even to Middle and South America. The truth is that no one can yet state precisely where the Cherokee came from. They speak Iroquois and may well have accompanied the Iroquoian themselves on their travels, possibly from a southwestern source into the Ohio Valley and then further east. The Cherokee left the mother group — glottochronology supports a date of 3,500 years ago for this event — moved south into Virginia and ultimately into the mountain country of southern Appalachia. There are archaeologists, however, who support an even greater time-depth for the Appalachia arrival (5 000 B.C.); there are those who believe that the Cherokee did not arrive until 1000-1300 A.D. Whatever the origins De Soto and his conquistadores did find a viable culture among the Cherokee when they arrived in 1540.

The Spaniards, and the English who followed, discovered that the Cherokee were town dwellers who farmed. Their relatively isolated settlements straddled the affluents of the upper Savannah, upper Coosa and Chattahoochee, and Little Tennessee and Hiwassee rivers. Their fields hugged low-lying canebrakes, flat valley floors and the slopes of the Blue Ridge and Great Smoky Mountains. On an earthen mound the Cherokee, who had seven clans, erected the dome-shaped, seven-sided Town House which dominated the village. A Town House might accommodate as many as 500 people. It served as a gathering place for religious ceremonials, councils held by the leaders, and for winter dancing. Nearby were the chunkey yard, the field where games such as lacrosse were played, the public granary, and the community gardens. Beyond these stood the small rectangular gable-roofed houses made of logs stripped of their bark, plastered with clay, and roofed with the bark of the chestnut.

While the Cherokee were sedentary agriculturalists (the women did the farming), they also relied heavily upon fishing, gathering and hunting for their livelihood. They fished with hook and line and spear, constructed the weir, and knew the art of fish poisoning. They gathered wild fruits, nuts, and berries in season. They pursued deer, bear, beaver, opossum, and wild turkey with bow and arrow and small game with blowgun, trap, or snare.

The Cherokee existed in an alternating state of war and peace. Bravery in battle was the chief criterion by which a boy was judged a man. And warriors sought action as far away as Florida and New York when no immediate neighbor threatened their destruction. Cherokee villages were ever mindful of war-peace dimensions. Factions of each — Red for war and White for peace — were present in every village. Both factions had their leaders. The Red, who had acquired the symbols of bravery — the wolf, fox, and owl — in battle; the White, who could invoke the spirits to remove the ills of their people. White leaders were considered sacred; they were separated as a class and were considered superior to and held apart from the rest of the community. They conducted the ordinary affairs of state. During times of war, however, Red voices rang out loudly throughout the Appalachian hills.

Warfare was chronic as English settlement in the Carolinas pressed the coastal tribes westward into Cherokee country. Before long English traders were operating among the Cherokee themselves. They brought guns, stroud cloth, metal goods, beads, and mirrors to the Lower, Middle, Valley, and Overhills villages. In 1738 smallpox struck the Cherokee and eliminated nearly half the population. Some warriors, disfigured by the disease, even took their own lives.

The warfare persisted during the colonial period. Cherokee villages were burned and

crops destroyed. Men, women, and children were sold into slavery. In 1761 smallpox struck again. For the Cherokee there was no respite. During the Revolutionary War they had sided with the British and were badly beaten. Fifty Cherokee towns were burned; most of their fields were destroyed; their finest warriors lay dead and their women and children were near starvation.

But the Cherokee held firm. Warfare had brought them closer together. The Red chiefs had taken over the reins of government. The Cherokee became adept at using the trader's gun; they began to use the new metal tools in agricultural pursuits and they took to raising horses and hogs. The old Town House was replaced by one circular in form. The old

habitations were replaced by one-, two-, and three-story log cabins. And into the Cherokee world came the Negro slave.

On November 28, 1785, the Cherokee entered into their first treaty arrangement with the United States. They ceded all of their lands east of the Blue Ridge as well as their Watauga and Cumberland River settlements to the Federal Government. Although their remaining lands were protected by the treaty American encroachment continued. As a result one Red faction left the Cherokee country to become the Chickamaugas. New agricultural implements were introduced with the intent that under Federal auspices the Cherokee warriors would become farmers. Some did but many others moved west. Be-

tween 1785 and 1817 some 2,000 made the westward trek.

Meanwhile the pace of acculturation had quickened. Moravian missionaries established the first mission school (1801) and others soon followed. Intermarriage had begun to produce a crop of well-educated mixed-bloods who were to become Cherokee leaders. They constituted a landed gentry and were slave-holders who built fine farmsteads rivaling those of the southern planters. One such leader was John Ross. Another perhaps was George Gist or Sequoyah.

Sequoyah, after twelve years of work, perfected a syllabary of eighty-six symbols, the so-called "talking leaves," by which the Cherokee were to learn to read and write in their own tongue. Although much ridiculed for his early attempts Sequoyah succeeded. The syllabary became the means by which several thousand Cherokee learned to read and write in a few short months. They could now keep records, write to their friends in the west, and even hope for a national literature, and a national academy. As a direct result of Sequoyah's work the *Cherokee Phoenix,* a newspaper with Elias Boudinot as editor, was first published on February 21, 1828.

Despite their cultural achievements and growing economic prosperity the Cherokee were in deep trouble in the 1820's and 30's. The Georgians in particular were determined to have the Cherokee lands and they pressed hard for Indian removal. The Cherokee, of course, were equally determined to remain. When gold was discovered on Cherokee land near Dahlonega, Georgia, a swarm of white adventurers quickly occupied the site. The Georgians immediately claimed that the Cherokee lands rightfully belonged to the State of Georgia. They served notice that the Cherokee lands would be disposed of by lottery. The Federal Government did not come to the aid of the Cherokee and the Indian Removal Act was signed by President Andrew Jackson on May 28, 1830.

The Cherokee fought back hard. John Ross led a delegation to Washington in the winter of 1832-1833 to plead the cause of his people but to no avail. The Treaty of New Echota was signed (1835) by a small unauthorized group. Under it the Cherokee were to receive seven million acres in the northeastern part of Oklahoma, in the Cherokee Strip, and in Kansas. The Cherokee responded by petition. They did not want to move.

Finally in 1838 General Winfield Scott with 7,000 troops began to round up the dissident Cherokee. Men, women, and children were herded into camps awaiting removal. John Ross suggested that the 1,000-mile migration wait until autumn rather than move his people in the heat of summer. He also suggested that the Cherokee themselves direct the migration. General Scott agreed. In bands of approximately 1,000, led by two able leaders, the Cherokee began to leave their homeland. In wagons, on horseback and on foot they moved northwest across Tennessee into Kentucky. They crossed the Ohio River at Golconda, Illinois, and the ice-clogged Mississippi near Cape Girardeau, Missouri. The last contingent — some 13,000 had started the trip — arrived in Indian Territory on March 26, 1839. It had truly been a "Trail of Tears." One-quarter of the 13,000 had not survived.

The Cherokee factions in the west (the old settlers, the John Ross supporters, the anti-John Ross group) did not come to an immediate understanding. The Civil War further divided the Cherokee. But in the war's aftermath the Cherokee rallied once more. By 1880, under Dennis Wolf Bushyhead, they had become relatively prosperous farmers, ranchers, and storekeepers. Their educated men were ministers, teachers, doctors, and lawyers. White settlement, however, could not be deterred and the western portion of the

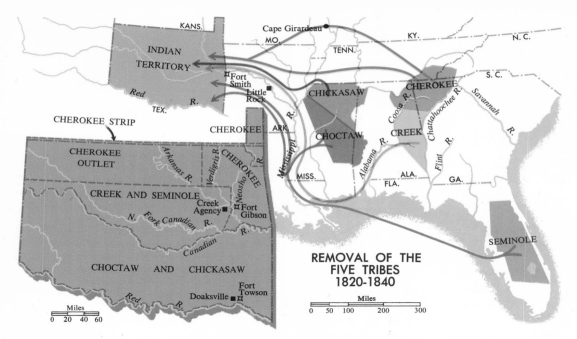

INDIAN TERRITORY

KANS.

Cape Girardeau

MO.

KY.

N. C.

TENN.

Fort Smith

Little Rock

CHICKASAW

CHEROKEE

S. C.

Red R.

TEX.

CHEROKEE

ARK.

Coosa R.

Savannah R.

CHEROKEE STRIP

CHEROKEE OUTLET

Arkansas R.

Verdigris R.

CHEROKEE

CHOCTAW

CREEK

Chattahoochee R.

Flint R.

CREEK AND SEMINOLE

Creek Agency

Fort Gibson

Neosho R.

Mississippi R.

MISS.

Alabama R.

ALA.

GA.

FLA.

N. Fork Canadian R.

Canadian R.

CHOCTAW AND CHICKASAW

Doaksville

Fort Towson

SEMINOLE

REMOVAL OF THE FIVE TRIBES 1820-1840

Miles
0   20   40   60

Miles
0   50   100   200   300

Cherokee lands were gradually invaded. In 1889 the land-hungry "Boomers" pushed into the Cherokee Strip, and on September 16, 1893, homesteading white men began to occupy the Cherokee Outlet.

But the Cherokee were not to be denied. As a result of deliberations with the Dawes Commission Cherokee tribal land was allotted in severalty although many of the full-bloods resisted the action. Every man, woman, and child was permitted to select an allotment of 110 acres; the land remaining was sold to the United States Government. When Oklahoma became a state (1907) the Cherokee, who had participated actively in its development, took part in the celebration. They have been active in Oklahoma affairs ever since. Approximately 14,000 Western Cherokee live in Oklahoma today.

All of the Cherokee, of course, did not submit to the "Trail of Tears." An obstinate band of perhaps 1,000 fled to the hills of western North Carolina. Unable under North Carolina law to purchase land, a white-trader friend of the Cherokee, Col. William H. Thomas, purchased it for them in *his* name. With Thomas' help the Cherokee divided their acreage into five districts: Bird Town, Paint Town, Wolf Town, Big Cove, and Yellow Hill. By 1848 population stood at 2,133. When Confederate Col. Thomas became ill and bankrupt following the Civil War

there was danger that the Cherokee would lose their tribal lands. To forestall such an occurrence the Cherokee adopted a constitution in 1875 so that they could transact business directly with the United States. The following year the Qualla Boundary or Reservation was established.

For the remainder of the 19th century there was little progress in the status of the Eastern Cherokee. They remained relatively isolated; the changes among them were few. The opening of Great Smoky Mountains National Park, and the concomitant development of roads and tourism, however, helped to break down the isolation. So, too, did public education.

Today the Eastern Cherokee support themselves largely by working in reservation forests and manufacturing plants (textiles, leathercrafts, and hair-styling accessories). Incomes are supplemented by working in traditional handicraft industries and through tourism. Small numbers in the remote areas still cling, however, to subsistence farming. But by and large the Eastern Cherokee have a new and fresh look. The Boundary Tree Tribal Motel Enterprise glistens in the summer sun, the schools are modern in every sense of the word, and the people themselves in the spirit of Sequoyah — 90% literate and over 5,500 strong — certainly not without problems — have arrived in the 20th century.

Seminole

Southeast

When the Spanish conquistadores arrived (Narváez, 1528 and De Soto, 1539) Florida was the home of the Apalachee, the Timucua, and Calusa Indians. The Spaniards were stunned by the fortified village sites, the quantities of food in the storehouses, and the number of Indians. Ocali, a Timucuan village near present-day Silver Springs, boasted six hundred dwellings and a population of several thousand. The population of the peninsula may well have exceeded twenty-five thousand.

But chronic warfare, diseases introduced by the Spanish conquerors, and later incursions upon the peninsula by South Carolinians and Georgians all but destroyed the Indian population. When the Lower Creeks made raids into northern Florida in the early 18th century they moved against towns whose inhabitants were barely able to defend themselves. They often dragged off the defenders as slaves.

The Spaniards attempted to attract Indian settlers to the Florida no-man's-land. They built Ft. San Marcos de Apalache at St. Marks and a trading post at Apalache (1744). But their gifts were not enough to induce the Lower Creeks to move to the peninsula. However, the Oconee, themselves Lower Creeks, had already begun to move on their own; they settled on the Alachua Prairie (1739-1750). One of their villages, Cuscowilla, was favored by thirty dwellings and several hundred inhabitants and under chief Cowkeeper they raised cattle and horses. Hitchiti-speaking peoples, pressed hard by Georgia whites, also pushed into northern Florida. And after 1750 larger numbers of Muskhogean-speaking Creeks began to move into Florida, no longer a vacuum. They built their towns in the Creek manner, on the Apalachicola and Suwannee rivers, near Tallahassee, the state capital, and on the Alachua Prairie.

But the Florida-Georgia borderland was in flames. The Georgians raided the Indian settlements, burned the fields, carried off the material goods, and captured the so-called "runaway" Negro slaves who had found refuge among the Indians. In retaliation the new Floridians occasionally struck the Georgia communities, but by 1800 they were being pressed west and south. Several villages were already standing on Tampa Bay and hunting forays were being made into south Florida. The raids continued during the War of 1812. In 1813 soldiers from Tennessee and Georgia burned 386 Indian houses, seized 2,000 bushels of maize, and carried off 300 horses and 400 head of cattle. After the defeat of the Creeks at Horseshoe Bend (1814) the Florida population swelled with refugees. One thousand Upper Creeks under Peter McQueen and Francis the Prophet moved into the Pensacola area. Tallapoosa and Coosa remnants moved to the Suwannee River. The Muskhogean-speaking Creeks were becoming the dominant population element in Florida. These then were the *Es-te se-mi-no-lee,* the "wild people," the Seminoles, Oconee, the Hitchiti-speakers, the Lower and Upper Creeks, other Indian groups, whites, and Negro runaway slaves.

Especially exasperating to the Southern whites were the Negro runaways. Exasperating, too, was the fact that Florida was still a Spanish possession. In 1818, accompanied by his volunteers, Andrew Jackson cut a fearsome swath across northern Florida (First Seminole War). The Seminoles fell back, disappearing among the thickets and entangling vines. Nearby Suwannee Indians and Negroes both appeared on Jackson's flanks. His troops were only saved by reinforcements hastily called up. Jackson put the torch to abandoned Suwannee as the Seminoles pushed farther south. Leaving his antagonists to his Creek allies Jackson swept down on Pensacola, captured the city, and established an American garrison there. The following year (1819) Uncle Sam purchased Florida from Spain for $5 million.

and kept in constant turmoil as the Seminole retreated, attacked and retreated once more. But the burden was too great. Virtually destitute, the worn-out and beaten Indians boarded the ships at Tampa Bay for the trip west. As many as 4,000 may have made the journey. Only 300 were left in Florida. In 1855 the Seminole in the peninsula numbered but 150.

In Oklahoma the Seminole, in 1856, were granted a tract of land separate and west of the Creeks. They survived the bitter dissension of the Civil War, in which they could be found on both sides. The Seminole Nation was formed in 1869.

The western Seminole remained town dwellers. Their homes were log cabins loosely clustered together. The former warriors became much more involved in agriculture, in tending livestock, in working on buildings and roads. The women cultivated their gardens and cared for the household. Missionaries moved into the Oklahoma lands. Schools were built. Relative isolation broke down in 1896 when the Choctaw, Oklahoma, and Gulf Railroad passed through Seminole territory. Prior to land allotment in 1903 there were fourteen towns represented in the tribal council of the Seminole Nation with a population numbering twenty-one hundred. In 1906 the Seminole Nation was dissolved.

Meanwhile, back in Florida in 1880, two hundred and eight Seminole were living in five widely scattered settlements. The largest of these was the Big Cypress Swamp settlement southwest of Lake Okeechobee. The typical house there and elsewhere was open-sided, supported a palmetto-thatched roof, and was built on a platform elevated three feet from the ground. On the rich hammocks the Seminole raised corn, sweet potatoes, beans, and melons. They gathered bananas, processed sugar cane, and the *koonti* root, from which they manufactured a yellow-white flour. They ate their fill of oranges, limes, lemons,

American settlers, mostly Southerners, began to move to Florida. Enthusiasm by Southerners and Creeks for the capture of Negro slaves continued unabated. The Seminoles, their backs to the wall, were pressed into the Treaty of Payne's Landing (1832), one of the provisions of which called for Seminole removal to the West. There were those who would go. There were others, who standing with Osceola, would never leave their Florida, never go to the Creek lands in the West, never give up the Negroes who were their friends and allies. The Seminoles resisted (Second Seminole War, 1835-1842), and under Osceola, Wildcat, Alligator, Arpeika, Tiger Tail, and Halek, kept the United States Army at bay. General Thomas S. Jesup's troops, perhaps 8,000 strong, were harassed

Map labels:
MISS.
CREEK INVASIONS 1700–1750
OCONEE
ALA.
FLA.
HITCHITI
Atlantic
Pensacola
GA.
Apalache (Tallahassee)
St. Marks
APALACHEE
TIMUCUA
Apalachicola R.
Apalachee Bay
Cuscowilla
Alachua Prairie
St. Augustine
Ocean
Suwannee R.
Ocali
Payne's Landing
Gulf of
Tampa
Tampa Bay
Bartow
Mexico
Ft. Meade
Brighton
L. Okeechobee
Ft. Myers
Big Cypress Swamp
Dania
TIMUCUA — Florida Indians prior to 1700
Seminole Indian area about 1830
Tamiami Trail
Miami
CALUSA
Everglades

grapes, pineapples and coconuts. They hunted with the Kentucky rifle, fished with hook and line and bow and arrow, raised cattle, swine, chickens, and horses. They purchased much of their clothing and bedding from white man's shops in Bartow, Fort Myers, Miami, Ft. Meade, and Tampa. They made flat baskets from swamp cane and palmetto stalks. They recognized at least nine clans, a head chief, and medicine man, and once each year participated in the Green Corn Dance at Fish-Eating Creek.

By 1912 the Oklahoma Seminole communities — those which retained the public square — had been reduced to six. But the Seminole population itself had already become more widely dispersed. The trend continued through the years as white contacts, resulting in loss of land and intermarriage, became increasingly prevalent. In the oil boom of the 20's, for example, few Seminole profited; the Indian lands had passed largely to white owners. Even more ominous for the Oklahoma Seminoles' future — the Indian population was beginning to lose its Indian identity.

Not so in Florida. There the Seminoles remained relatively isolated until the late 20's. In 1928 U.S. Highway 41, the Tamiami Trail, was completed through the wilderness. The highway and urban growth along Florida's southeast coast ended forever the Seminoles' isolation. By 1941 many of Florida's Seminoles were living on three reservations: Brighton, just northwest of Lake Okeechobee; Big Cypress, south and west of the lake; and Dania, twenty miles north of Miami. Others lived on land set aside by the State of Florida. But more than half chose to build their villages on non-reservation lands, on tracts northeast of Lake Okeechobee, in the Big Cypress Swamp west of the reservation, and at random locations along the Tamiami Trail. By 1950 Seminole population had soared to eight hundred and twenty-three; in 1960 one

thousand and three were recorded in the Seminole Agency; in 1969 the estimate was approximately fifteen hundred.

While the present-day Seminoles still waver between acceptance and rejection of the white man's world, they have already accepted a great part of it. They have become wage laborers. Many Seminoles work off the reservations on nearby cattle ranches and vegetable farms. They sell handmade dolls, beadwork, and clothing at sidewalk camps. The dugout canoe has been replaced by the factory-manufactured canoe and the air boat. Today's open-air or one-room houses contain white man's cooking utensils, sewing machines, and phonographs. The automobile is a common sight among them. Seminole children are attending both reservation schools and Florida's public schools. Hospitals, doctors, and public health officials cater to Seminole needs.

But everything does not change. The Brighton reservation medicine man still keeps the medicine bundle — the soul of the Seminole in his possession. He guards it well. The medicine in it he knows is alive. If the medicine is permitted to die, life itself would pass from the tribe. During each year's Green Corn Dance the medicine man stands in a pond facing east. He rubs water over his body and prays that he can handle the medicine safely and for the good of his people.

The Seminole is changing; he is also holding on. Fifteen hundred strong in Florida; over 2,300 strong in Oklahoma.

Mandan

Prairies

The eastward flowing tributaries — the White, Cheyenne, Moreau, Grand, Cannonball, Heart, and Knife rivers — all are western Dakota feeders of the muddy Missouri. By the 13th century A.D. migrant Indian groups were moving up the mighty river and spilling over into a number of the tributaries. In the two centuries that followed clusters of villages, featuring rectangular semi-subterranean earth lodges, sprang up on the high terraces overlooking the rivers themselves. In the bottomlands the villagers planted maize, squash, and beans. On the grassland between the rivers they hunted the bison, probably their chief food source, and the antelope, deer, elk, badger, rabbit, and raccoon. As Indian groups continued to push into the upper Missouri Valley they added to the already existing villages; they even helped to spawn new ones. In historic times the descendants of these prosperous villagers would be known to the world as the Mandan.

The Western World would know them initially as skillful traders. For it was to the Mandan villages that the tribes farther north and east (Assiniboin, Cree, Sioux) brought the wares obtained from the Europeans: guns and powder, axes, knives, and kettles. The western or plains tribes brought carefully dressed bison and deer hides as well as quantities of furs. The products of east and west were exchanged through the middlemen, the Mandan, who provided all comers with the bounty of their country, their surplus of agricultural products. The Assiniboin, using a well-established trail, had been coming to the Mandan villages for some years when in 1738 they were joined by the French trader-explorer Pierre Gaultin de Varennes de La Vérendrye.

In La Vérendrye's day the Mandan no longer lived in small scattered villages. Their 10,000 people had been reorganized in nine large towns near the Heart-Missouri confluence. Enemy assaults, particularly from the Sioux, had made consolidation frightfully necessary. The towns were now fortified, replete with bastions, moats, and palisades. The settlement pattern itself had changed considerably. No longer, for example, was the rectangular earth-lodge home visible, although a remnant remained in the rectangular ceremonial lodge. Earth-lodge homes were now circular in form in imitation apparently of their Arikara neighbors. They were set up along "streets" around a central square. The Mandan continued to be agriculturalists and sometime hunters. They stored their surpluses in pits and caches in and beyond the towns. And to cope with problems of survival they certainly had by La Vérendrye's day forged a new set of social institutions. They had organized in moieties and clans, adopted an age-grade system through which the males passed, and developed a rich and viable ceremonial system.

In the aftermath of La Vérendrye's visit, traders, from established companies as well as independents, visited the Mandan towns. Their prime interest was in the fur trade. Unfortunately for the Mandan, however, they brought with them the white man's diseases. Smallpox struck in 1764 and again in 1781. The Mandan towns reeled under the impact. To add to the horror, the Teton Sioux moving west to the plains attacked the towns and virtually destroyed them. The survivors, forced to abandon Heart River, moved north and founded two villages on the right bank of the Missouri just south of Knife River and just south of their Hidatsa neighbors. When John Evans, searching for the "Welsh Indians," wintered in the Mandan villages (1796-1797), they numbered but 1,520. Lewis and Clark, during their own memorable winter stay (1804-1805) estimated the two-village population at 1,250. Twenty-eight years later (1832), when George Catlin made their acquaintance, they numbered about 1,700.

Catlin, the far-famed painter of Indian scenes and portraits (many of them Mandan) left the first account of the most important Mandan ceremonial, the *okipa*. The four-day ceremonial, held in summer, was maintained in an effort to keep the Mandan conscious of their origin (they were created by Lone Man) and their history; it was during the okipa that the bull dance, designed to lure the bison to the Mandan country, was held. It was during the okipa, too, that the young men approaching manhood went, in Catlin's words:

"...through an ordeal of privation and bodily torture, which while it was supposed to harden their muscles and prepare them for extreme endurance, enabled their chiefs, who were spectators to the scene, to decide upon their comparative bodily strength, and ability to endure the privations and sufferings that often fall to the lot of Indian warriors, and that they might decide who amongst the young men was the best able to lead a war-party in an extreme exigency."

The okipa was designed, therefore, to perpetuate the Mandan as a people; it was also designed to help perpetuate the Mandan culture. In 1837 the Mandan were to receive a blow of major proportions. It would test whether or not people and culture would live or die. The smallpox once more! Victims died literally by the hundreds. Their bodies were thrown from the bluff at Fort Clark (near the Mandan villages) to the riverbank. As the days passed the stench became unbearable. Suicide was prevalent. Four Bears, before dying of the disease himself, asked the living warriors to seek vengeance upon the white man, who had brought the disease to the villages. But the Mandan could muster no strength. Eighty percent of their people lay dead. Twenty adult men, forty adult women, and approximately seventy children survived the epidemic. And they were yet to face the

battle-strong Sioux, who in their hatred would burn one of the Mandan villages; the Arikara would occupy the other. In 1845, when the Hidatsa moved upstream to Like-a-Fish-Hook Village, the Mandan survivors joined them.

The Mandan only occupied one portion of Like-a-Fish-Hook Village. The Hidatsa and Arikara occupied other sections. In their portion the Mandan attempted to resurrect their old settlement pattern. They allowed room for the central plaza, built their ceremonial lodge, and fenced the area with a stockade. They planted maize, hunted when possible, traded with the nomadic Indian tribes, and sold hides to the fur companies. They maintained the clan system (despite the loss of a number of clans) and continued to perform a number of their ceremonials including the okipa. But they could not maintain the pace. In the late 1860's famine stalked the Like-a-Fish-Hook Village. The Mandan could survive only through govern-

Crow

ment aid. The Mandan had reached a new low.

In 1882 the exodus from Like-a-Fish-Hook Village was begun. The Mandan were among the very last to leave. Lands were allotted to them on the Fort Berthold Reservation — 160 acres to each family head, 80 acres to all others. The Mandan were settled in seven villages, but large Hidatsa and Arikara populations were represented in each. One might say for the Mandan and Hidatsa (they had frequently intermarried) that they had merged — were in fact one. They were wards of the federal government.

But the final blow was yet to come. The Garrison Dam! The earth-filled structure, 202-feet high, was slung across the Missouri River in the late 1940's and early 1950's. At full pool it would inundate more than 320,000 acres of North Dakota bottomland, impound the Missouri's water to the Montana state line, and divide the Fort Berthold Reservation into five distinct segments. Most serious of all it would call for the relocation of the Indian people themselves. In 1950-1951 fifty community meetings were held on the reservation to discuss relocation. What would happen to the land, the schools, the roads, the Indian agency? By 1952 relocation was in full motion as the tribesmen moved from the rich tree-covered bottomland to the treeless prairie. While many relocated on the reservation itself, others simply left. By the end of 1954 relocation had been completed. And in the succeeding decade new houses, new roads, new schools and a new Indian agency (at New Town) were all in process of creation or growth. On the face of the land the new developments all looked well. But what had happened to the Indian in the process? To his self-concept? To his well being?

Smallpox, 1837. Abandonment of Like-a-Fish-Hook Village, 1882. Garrison Dam and relocation, the 1950's. What, Lone Man, have your people wrought?

52

Plains

Traditions indicate that the Crow lived at one time in the Hidatsa country near the Missouri-Knife River confluence. They were farmers and sometime hunters. They lived in the traditional earth lodge. When an argument over the ownership of the upper stomach of a bison could not be resolved (two women from two different clans battled each other and one was ultimately killed), one faction of the tribe under No Vitals left the Hidatsa village and moved north and west along the Missouri's left bank. In the late 17th or early 18th century the migrants crossed the Missouri and wandered south onto the rolling grassland between the "Big Muddy" and the Yellowstone. During their wanderings they acquired horses, and as mounted warriors they contested with the Shoshone for the wide plain, deep valley, and high mountain country south of the Yellowstone. They were obviously victorious. The Absaroke, or children of the Large-Beaked Bird, as they called themselves (the French-speaking fur traders referred to them as *gens de corbeaux*, hence Crow) were to occupy the land between the lower Yellowstone and the distant Wind River Range. They were to become full-fledged Plains Indians.

The Crow treasured especially the land just east of the Rocky Mountain frame which Edwin T. Denig, the fur trader, called ". . . the best game country in the world." Hundreds of elk and deer drank their fill in the rivers, beaver were plentiful, and fish and fowl abundant. Antelope darted over the grassland. In the mountain country grizzly bear and bighorn sheep were readily available. But for the Crow and other Plains Indians, it was the great swarm of bison which blanketed the grassland in summer that made life in the Crow country livable and indeed worthwhile.

In the early summer when the grass was high and the bison had congregated in herds the Crow, too, came together. Families and bands emerged from their protective winter quarters in the mountains or deep valleys and moved to a prearranged rendezvous. They assembled their *tipis,* or skin tents, three or four deep, in a huge camp circle open only toward the east. The clans—the Sore-lip Lodge, Whistling Water, Kicked-in-the-Bellies, and others—occupied particular places on the circle. Thirty-five hundred Crow, in 350 tipis, a quarter of a mile around—truly a sight to behold!

It was in the camp circle that the summer bison hunt was planned. The camp leader, aided by the military club leaders and camp herald, made the necessary arrangements. On their well-trained and well-fed horses the Crow made their approach. They rode round and round the herd firing their arrows at will. The bison, thrown into utter confusion by the "surround," could not withstand the onslaught. They lay mortally wounded on the summer grass.

Then the Crow women, often assisted by the children, went to work on the bison carcasses. They separated the skins from the body, cut the meat in thin slivers, and hung them on racks to dry. They also collected cherries and other wild fruits, added bison fat, bone marrow, as well as the dried bison meat and pounded the mass (they used a stone maul encased in rawhide) into a concoction known on the plains as *pemmican,* the staple in the diet of all the Plains Indians. Pemmican was often stored in the *parfleche,* the handy rawhide receptacle which could easily be slung across a horse's back or packed on a horse or dog *travois.*

While hunting was a prime necessity for the Crow, waging war was, perhaps, of equal significance. For the Crow was first and foremost a warrior, reared as such from childhood. Long had he heard about war honors, of collecting *coups,* or striking blows against

Crow enemies. Long had he heard about taking revenge for the deaths of brother clansmen at the hands of Blackfoot or Sioux. Long had he heard that death on the battlefield was most honorable, a way to join the gods. Long had he sought a vision to obtain the "medicine" that would make him a noble warrior—a noble Crow.

A vision seeker, seeking revenge for a dead clan brother, might call for the Sun Dance, perhaps the most important of the Crow ceremonials. Sponsored by a shaman who held the sacred bundle, the vision seeker would dance, sing, and pray in a specially built tipi. He was often joined by others. Together they would dance, endure pain, and fast. To the vision finder, of course, would come all of the Crow glories. And while the principals were engaged in vision-seeking other tribesmen participated in numerous social events: they played dice games, ran races, planned weddings, and held meetings. The Sun Dance was often the social highlight of the Crow year.

53

Comanche

But for most of the year, except in winter, the Crow were on the move. They traveled north by way of the Powder and Tongue rivers to the lower Yellowstone, then west to the Musselshell and south once more to their winter encampments near the Absaroka and Wind River ranges. On their travels they occasionally visited the white man's fur trading posts. But intimate contact was only slight. Unfortunately for the Crow the wandering was not to last. By the terms of the Fort Laramie Treaty, May 7, 1868, the Absaroke relinquished all of the lands for which they had given their blood, and accepted the reservation. Their new home, in the heart of the old homeland, extended from the 107th meridian west to near the Clark Fork of the Yellowstone, and from the Wyoming state line almost north to the Yellowstone itself. While Sioux and Blackfoot raiders continued to harass them for some years it was quite plain to the Crow that the old life was passing. By 1888 the bison were no more and the need for counting coups had virtually passed. In 1904 the Department of the Interior banned the Sun Dance—but the need for it, too, had long since vanished. Although revived once more in 1941 (it was brought to the Crow by the Wind River Shoshone) with the self-torture element removed, the ceremony was in reality only a shadow of its former self.

The "new" continued to arrive. In 1961 the Crow were awarded $9 million by the Federal Government in lieu of lands ceded by them in the 19th century. The money was used largely to repair or remodel old houses or to build entirely new ones. It bought cattle and land. In 1963 the tribe received $2 million in compensation for tribal lands taken for the Yellowtail Dam and Reservoir. And in summer 1969 the Crow were talking about pursuing the future by building a community college on the Indian reservation.

Plains

The "wild" Comanche, the horse-stealing marauders of the southern plains (18th and 19th centuries), stemmed from peaceful origins. In the early 17th century their small bands, and those of their linguistic brethren — the Ute and Shoshone — ever in search of food, roamed the Great Basin. They snared jackrabbits and gathered wild seeds, nuts, roots, and berries. They lived in small huts or lean-tos. So rigorous was their food quest that they had precious little time for ceremonials, for political organization, or for war. Continuous wandering was to lead many of the bands into the mountain country of Colorado, to the "parks," and ultimately to the Great Plains. There the Ute were already forging friendly relations with Apache and Navajo in the late 17th century (in the absence of the Spaniards during the Pueblo

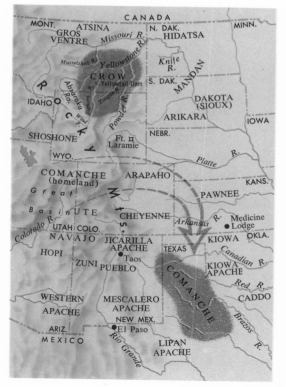

revolt of 1680-1692), and together they raided Taos and other pueblos. So successful were they that they invited their Comanche kinsmen south. The Yamparike (the Spanish Llamparicas), for example, the very first Comanche band to appear on the plains, left the Colorado park country, pushed through the Front Range of the Rockies (c. 1700), and joined the Ute in raiding the rich pueblos.

The Ute-Comanche also raided the Apache *rancherías* on the plains. They stole into the settlements, struck the men down, set fire to the huts and crops, and carried away the women and children, many of whom would be disposed of at the slave mart in Taos. They also ran off with the horses. By 1719 as tipi-dwelling, bison-hunting, and horse-using Indians, the Ute-Comanche moved freely across the plains. They exchanged horses for French guns with the Pawnee in the east; they traded bison meat and skins for maize, vegetables, blankets, and Spanish knives and hatchets at the Taos fair; and they occasionally struck the pueblos in hit-and-run raids. In 1749, however, the Comanche suddenly turned on their Ute brothers (scholars do not know why) and drove them from the Great Plains. By 1755 the Ute had been pushed back into the Rockies. The Comanche bands meanwhile had turned south, masters of their future, to the Red River and beyond.

In the third decade of the 19th century the Comanche bands occupied the southern plains from the Arkansas River to the Mexican settlements. Their encampments could often be found near the headwaters of the larger streams, in the "breaks" or arroyos, where grass, wood for their fires, and water were available. There was no established settlement pattern. The tipis might be arranged in a rough circle, in a rectangular plan, or simply strung along the stream bank. But the bands did not remain long in one place. The Kutsueka (Kotsoteka), or Bison Eaters, for

example, were especially dependent upon the movements of the bison. They followed the herds south from the Canadian River in fall and north toward the river in late spring. In summer they set up a temporary camp to prepare for the communal hunt.

Near a fine water and timber supply the women set up the tipis and erected racks for drying bison strips. On the appointed day the hunt leader led his mounted band against the bison. The approach was made in a great semicircle, downwind. Slowly but surely the hunters moved around the herd. Each man was on his own as he poured arrows into the bison's vitals. The highly individualistic Comanche were known at times to charge the herds on horseback, lances in hand, and using both hands plunge the weapon into the bison's heart. Nor did the Comanche wait for their women to butcher the animals. They proceeded to the task themselves. The communal hunt was followed by the Bison Tongue Feast, a feature of which was a midday meal served by a woman of virtue.

But even a virtuous woman compared unfavorably with a favorite horse. For the Comanche held the horse in the highest esteem. A horse might serve as a gift for a bride, a fee for a shaman's aid, or a means of exchange. Wealth to the Comanche meant wealth in horses. A wealthy member of the Kweharenuh (Kwahari), or Antelope Band, might well own over 1,000 horses. Capturing or stealing horses, therefore, became a Comanche prerogative. Raids for horses were made well into the pueblo country and deep into Mexico. A number of the bands made it a practice to capture the wild mustang at waterholes or in specially built corrals. They "broke" the animals and learned to ride and breed them. None on the plains could equal their skill.

But as time passed it became abundantly clear to the Comanche that Wolf, the creator,

or Coyote, the trickster, was playing games with the *nemena* (as the Comanche called themselves), for white men were pushing into the Comanche country and the bison herds did not seem to appear with their accustomed regularity. Between 1830 and 1860 it became increasingly difficult to feed the Comanche bands by hunting alone. The Comanche resorted once more to raiding and marauding. On August 25, 1868, by the terms of the Medicine Lodge Treaty, the Comanche, Cheyenne, Arapaho, Kiowa and Kiowa-Apache were assigned to reservation lands. According to the treaty they would refrain from attacking white settlements, they were to permit the building of rail lines and roads through their territory, they were to accept an agency, and were to be given tools which would enable them to farm the land. These for the Comanche, the mighty hunters, the "Lords of the South Plains."

So difficult was the adjustment, so scarce the food on the reservation in 1874, that the Comanche began to listen more and more to Ishatai, or Coyote Droppings. He it was who had the "medicine," he it was who had communed with the Great Spirit, and he it was who would lead the Comanche to a new and better life. Coyote Droppings called for the Sun Dance. And the people followed and believed. But in an attack upon Adobe Walls, Texas, on June 24, 1874, the medicine of Coyote Droppings proved less than effective. When the military moved into the Comanche-Kiowa country (1874-1875) the life of the past was all but over. The Comanche would be marauders no more.

Comanche reservation land was ultimately allotted. Those portions not used by the Indians were thrown open for settlement. When Oklahoma became a state (1907) the dream was that the Comanche would become part and parcel of the American people. That in fact has happened. Yet in 1962 the Kiowa Area Field Office could list Kiowa, Comanche and Apache numbers at 5,566. The nemena, as such, were still very much alive.

56

Nez Perce

Western Plateau

The monster filled the Kamiah Valley. His great hands reached out and swept the neighboring earth of visible animals. He devoured the beasts with positive relish. But Coyote could bear it no longer. He jumped into the monster's throat, agate knife in hand, and cut his heart and body into small pieces. These he dispatched to the distant plains and mountains to become the Indian tribes of history. But in the process the Kamiah Valley was left quite empty. Why not an Indian people for the Kamiah? For the entire Clearwater country? Coyote thought about it for only a moment. Then he took a few drops of the best blood from the monster's heart and created from the liquid the *nimapu*, the real people, the very finest people—the Nez Perce.

Archaeologists have only recently begun to work in the Nez Perce country. They still know little about Nez Perce beginnings. In caves along the Salmon and Snake rivers they have uncovered spear points, combs, and woven grasses that date back 4,000 years. These remains (and others) were undoubtedly left by precursors of the Nez Perce who had wandered south via the Fraser, Okanogan, and Columbia river valleys. In their new homeland the new arrivals built clusters of circular pit houses with flat earthen roofs, and sustained themselves by hunting in the neighboring forests and gathering wild roots, bulbs, and berries. As the centuries wore on the pit-house dwellers were joined from time to time by families and bands moving in from the north and west. House type and means of subsistence, however, changed but little. As late as the 13th century A.D. the forerunners of the Nez Perce were still principally engaged in hunting and gathering.

Late in the 13th century, as a result of the damming of the Columbia River by the Cascade Landslide, salmon could at long last move upstream beyond The Dalles. They began to establish spawning grounds in the Nez Perce country. Recognizing the salmon as a fine food resource the Indians proceeded to erect their dwellings (now semi-subterranean earth lodges covered with mats, reeds, or grasses) near the important salmon-bearing streams. With the passage of time they became expert salmon fishermen. After the salmon catch they would move from their river-oriented villages to the old hunting and gathering grounds. There they made camp, did some hunting, and gathered the bulbs of the camas plant. There is evidence, too, that they began a trading relationship with peoples near the distant Pacific.

It was from such beginnings that the Shahaptian-speaking Nez Perce emerged as a people. In the early 19th century (Lewis and Clark visited them in 1805 and 1806) the approximately 6,000 Nez Perce were dispersed in 60 to 70 independent villages in the Snake, Salmon, Clearwater, and Grand Ronde drainage basins. When spring burst upon the villages the women moved to the hillsides. They dug out the roots of the cowish plant with sharp digging sticks. The roots were either steamed and eaten or cooked in biscuit form and preserved. The men, meanwhile, were busy on the salmon-fishing platforms, dipping their nets into the swirling waters below. The women cut the captured salmon into slices which they hung on racks to dry. The dried slices were then beaten into a pulp and preserved as salmon pemmican.

In late summer the Nez Perce abandoned their river-clinging villages and moved up into the camas grounds. So abundant was the camas that it often required only four or five days' work to gather the year's supply. The Nez Perce, therefore, took advantage of the spare time to hunt, gamble, meet with old friends from other villages, play games, and race their horses near the camas grounds.

Horses had been part of the Nez Perce lifeway since 1720. They had probably been

obtained by theft from their Shoshone enemies. In Lewis and Clark's day the Nez Perce already owned large horse herds. They were successful breeders; they bred the Appaloosa—a significant trade item. They crossed the Rockies and sold horses to the Crow in exchange for bison skins, parfleches (gay containers), porcupine quills, and tobacco; they traveled to The Dalles emporium and gave up horses for *hiqua,* the shell that served as a medium of exchange in the Pacific Northwest. And more and more, individual tribesmen and small bands began to leave the Nez Perce country for the plains, where they adopted a number of new pursuits, including bison hunting and tipi building. These were introduced, of course, to the Nez Perce at home. The tipi began to replace the mat-covered earth lodge as the prime Nez Perce dwelling.

Many other changes were in store for the nimapu. In 1831 (through a delegation sent to St. Louis) the Nez Perce asked that teachers and missionaries be sent to the Clearwater. For the tribesmen knew that the written word contained powerful "medicine." Had not Spokane Garry created a sensation among *his* people when he had read passages from the Bible? Five years were to pass, however, before Henry H. Spalding and his wife were to take up the Nez Perce mission at Lapwai. They learned Shahaptian as a matter of course. Eliza Spalding then devised an alphabet expressing all of the Shahaptian sounds. As a result of her labors many of the Nez Perce learned to read and write in their own tongue. Several students were given instruction in English. Meanwhile, Spalding himself was introducing garden agriculture to the Nez Perce. Wheat, potatoes, and vegetables were the first crops raised. The Indians also learned to care for chickens, pigs, and sheep. The mission flourished until 1845 and then deteriorated (possibly due to Mrs.

Spalding's illness); it was finally abandoned in 1847.

Meanwhile the white man was moving ever westward. The Oregon Trail led him to the southern fringes of the Nez Perce country. The tribesmen, taking advantage of the situation, found it profitable to supply the wagon trains with their horses, salmon, meat, and camas. They even suggested diverting the traffic via the Little Salmon and Clearwater rivers, but without success. The white man continued to come. He began to settle in the areas long claimed by the Nez Perce. When Isaac Stevens was appointed Governor of Washington Territory and Indian agent for the Northwest, he proposed that the Indians be settled on a reservation before difficulties between the races led to outright war. At the council on the Walla Walla River (1855) the Nez Perce Reservation, including most of the old Nez Perce country, was defined.

In 1860 gold was discovered on the reservation. Miners and settlers, both eager to seize the opportunity, quickly moved into the reservation area. The Nez Perce could not stop the stampede. In 1863, at Lapwai, another council was held. But the Nez Perce were bitterly divided. One faction under Chief Lawyer was prepared to side with the government; a second faction under Big Thunder asked the government to enforce the treaty of 1855; a third faction led by Eagle from the Light would brook no compromise. The whites must be thrown out of the Nez Perce country. The treaty of 1863 was signed only by the Lawyer faction. The anti-treaty bands withdrew. Under the new treaty the Nez Perce Reservation was much reduced. Long held lands in the Snake, Salmon, Wallowa, and Grand Ronde valleys were literally taken from the tribesmen.

The anti-treaty forces were completely dismayed. White settlers began to push into the Grand Ronde and Wallowa valleys. There would be no peace. Dissident warriors took it upon themselves to flail the settlers; a number were killed. The killings paved the way for the abandonment by the Nez Perce of land in Oregon and Idaho, and for the war of 1877.

Under Looking Glass the Nez Perce started out over the Lolo Trail with General O.O. Howard in hot pursuit. The Nez Perce would go to the plains country where, hopefully, they would be received in peace by their friends, the Crow. They crossed into what is now Yellowstone National Park and swung north along Clark Fork (now determined to flee to Canada), but were caught by General Nelson A. Miles near the Bearpaw Mountains. With many of their war chiefs now dead and their people in absolute misery, the Nez Perce, under Chief Joseph, surrendered—87 men, 184 women, 147 children. One-hundred fifty-one Nez Perce were dead.

Chief Joseph and his party were sent as prisoners to Indian Territory. It was not until 1885 that they were returned to the Northwest—some to Lapwai, others, including Chief Joseph, to the Colville Reservation in Washington.

In 1895 the Nez Perce lands were allotted in severalty. The original reservation as such was no more. But during John Collier's tenure as Commissioner of Indian Affairs (beginning in 1933) the Nez Perce restored their tribal government. Funds and lands were to be held in common. In 1951, under the terms of the Indian Claims Commission Act, the Nez Perce filed a petition asking payment for lands ceded (and for gold taken) under the treaties of 1855 and 1863. The case was argued for years. But for their pains in the previous century the Nez Perce were finally awarded $7,650,000. The nimapu (1,500 in number today) had finally won the battle. But Coyote, can you not hear Chief Joseph stirring in his grave?

Paiute

Great Basin

The Humboldt River winds its way westward for nearly 300 miles across the face of Nevada before disappearing in the Humboldt Sink. Trickles of water then lead the traveler south to Carson Sink and on to the Walker River and Walker Lake. There are other water bodies too: Pyramid Lake, Owens River, and Owens Lake (now dry), in the western Great Basin. But these are anomalies, for between the towering Sierras and the Toiyabe Range of central Nevada, the country of the Northern Paiute, the earth for the most part lies parched and dry. The sun literally bakes the ground. Only near the summits of the north-south trending mountain ranges is precipitation conspicuous; there the piñon stands rise to the sky. On the semi-arid basin floors, on the other hand, sagebrush and creosote bush dominate. Upslope the grasses, porcupine and rye seed, and above them the juniper and willow thrive. Animal life, of course, is scanty. In aboriginal times rabbits and squirrels could be found on the basin floors, antelope and deer farther upslope, and mountain sheep and goats at the highest elevations. Only in the well-watered areas were swans, geese, ducks, and pelicans available. In the country of the Southern Paiute, the deserts of southwestern Utah, eastern California, northwestern Arizona, and southern Nevada, environmental conditions were even more extreme. There were fewer flowing streams and fewer plant and animal resources. For the *nimwin* ("the people") — the Paiute (both Northern and Southern) — procuring a living was most difficult at best.

In early spring Northern Paiute families left their *wickiups* (the winter dwellings made of juniper and willow poles, bent over, tied with bark strips, and covered with bark or grass) for the mountain slopes. While the men searched the grasses for seeds the women set up temporary dwellings and prepared for the gathering enterprise. Armed with knives, seed

beaters, and a variety of well-made baskets the women scoured the area. When Wolf the Good Brother was watching over them, the harvest was especially good. The gathered seeds were ground, mixed with chokeberry flour, and stored in pits at the winter settlement. There were years, however, when the porcupine grass and rye seeds did not appear; starvation then stalked the Paiute country.

There was little letup in the food quest. In the heat of summer, during the passage of grasshopper swarms, the Paiute filled the air with clubs in an effort to bring the insects down. Some families ate the catches raw; others threw them into pits and boiled them. Surpluses were often stored. In late summer when the edible roots began to mature the Paiute women dug them out carefully; they gathered wild berries during the same period. In autumn the Paiute went to the high slopes to gather the piñon nut—perhaps the Paiutes' most important food. The gathered nuts were carried in large burden baskets to the winter settlement. There they were crushed and stored in skin-lined pits.

In late autumn a number of families, sometimes even several bands, joined together in the sage-covered basins for a communal hunt. Low nets were set up in a huge semicircle near the waterholes. The Paiute hunters, armed with clubs, merely waited. When the rabbits charged the nets they were clubbed to death. A good meat supply was thereby assured, and from the hunt's product Paiute women made the fine rabbit skin blanket — a source of warmth for the Indian during the Great Basin's cold winter.

In every basin, in every isolated valley, life for the Paiute was somewhat different depending largely upon environmental conditions. Life was, perhaps, best in the well-watered Owens Valley where Paiute villages were clustered along stream banks and all essential food resources were located within

a radius of twenty miles. Owens Valley bands owned the territory over which they moved. Trespassing could lead to open fights. Each of the bands was led by a chief who directed the animal drives, looked after the erection of the village sweat lodge, conducted mourning ceremonies and festivals, and kept informed about the ripening of the piñon nuts. So sophisticated were the Owens Valley Paiute that they irrigated the native plants and carried on trade relations with the trans-Sierran Western Mono. For the Southern Paiute, of course, life was very different. They simply moved constantly from place to place in an effort to eke out an existence.

White settlement came late to the Paiute country. Escalante's visit to the Southern Paiute in 1776 made no impact whatever. Peter Skene Ogden, Jedediah Smith, and Joseph Walker, travelers in the Northern Paiute country (1826-1833), likewise made little impact. The remote basins and valleys were left completely untouched. But trappers, California gold seekers, and the discovery of the Comstock Lode (1859) northeast of Carson City, were to change the picture entirely. Miners and settlers began to pour into Nevada's rich mineral lands. Livestock were turned out to pasture in the Paiute hills, decimating the native food sources. White men cut down the piñon for fuel. In 1869 the transcontinental railroad was built across Paiute territory. The cultural shock produced by the newcomers was virtually electric. Some of the Paiute settled on ranches or in the mining communities. Others were satisfied with reservation status at Pyramid Lake, Walker River, or Owens River. There was desultory fighting, much drinking, and debauchery. Oblivion seemed to be in store for the Indian.

Then out of Mason Valley (present-day Yerington) came the voice of Wovoka, "the Cutter," son of a shaman, who taught the Paiute to harm no one, to live at peace with the white man, and to return to gathering the porcupine grass seed and the piñon nut as of old. Wovoka claimed that he had visited with God. He taught that the dead would be returned to life. He also taught the Paiute what came to be called the Ghost Dance. It spread like wildfire through Wovoka's disciples to the plains. The Sioux adopted the dance, but they did not preach the prophet's words. The Ghost Dance became a call to war. It was to result in the death of 300 Indians at Wounded Knee Creek, half of them women and children, on December 29, 1890.

Wovoka died in a small cabin in Nevada in 1932. But his people live on. They are scattered today over numerous reservations and "colonies," perhaps 3,000 in all. There are Paiute in Battle Mountain, in Lovelock and at Pyramid Lake and Walker Lake. There are Paiute in Yerington and in the Reno ghetto. Where to now, Wovoka?

Pomo

California

A long string of shell beads found in a dry cave in Nevada provides evidence for Indian occupation of central California some 9,000 years ago. Central Californians were at that time gathering marine shells on the coast, manufacturing beads, and distributing them through trade channels to the Coast Ranges, to the Central Valley, and over the high Sierras. California would ultimately become the home of over 100 separate tribes, including five linguistic stocks, a veritable cul-de-sac into which people moved from the north, east, and south. The food-laden lands of central California, for example, became the home of no fewer than eighteen tribes. At Clear Lake, in the Russian River drainage, and along the Pacific coast between Gualala River and Bodega Bay lived the Pomo.

The Clear Lake area was particularly well endowed with food resources. From their village communities near, around, and in the lake (Elem, Koi, and Kamdot were on

islands), or from temporary camps set up as occasions demanded, the Pomo pursued their food supply. In spring they fished the streams for hitch, suckers and blackfish, went to the mountain meadows for clover, and fished the lake from the tule balsa (reed rafts); in summer they moved to the hills for root gathering and to the lake fringes for tule and freshwater clams. Because salt was unavailable at Clear Lake trips were made to the coast in late summer for that commodity. The women and children at home, meanwhile, scoured the hills for seeds for pinole flour. In autumn, the most significant gathering season, the acorn, a Pomo staple, became the great attraction. Women, often assisted by the men and children (they frequently climbed the oaks and shook the acorns loose), all took part in the harvest. Winter found the Pomo balsa in the water once more, as the mudhen and other waterfowl were brought down with sling and adobe pellet. Elk and deer, a wide variety of small animals, pepperwood balls, cherries, and piñon nuts were all accessible to the Clear Lake Pomo. The environment was truly one of abundance.

Coyote, the Creator, provided less well for the Pomo of Russian River, and perhaps least well for the coastal Pomo. But famine was indeed rare. When the acorn supply failed at Clear Lake, traders would hasten to Russian River to procure a supply; the Russian River Pomo traveled regularly to the coast to gather seaweed, mussels, and clams; the Pomo of the coast could eke out a livelihood on wild oats, acorns, venison, roots, berries, fish and a variety of shellfish.

The Pomo village communities, as many as seventy in number, with a population of approximately 8,000 in the late 18th century, were completely autonomous. Each was headed by a chief, ordinarily a fine orator. The larger village communities had several sub-chiefs as well, the offices being not

necessarily hereditary. A typical village consisted of the dwellings of the tribesmen (dome-shaped and thatched with tule at Clear Lake; with grass near Russian River; cone-shaped and constructed with wood and redwood bark along the coast). There was also the circular semi-subterranean dance house where the ceremonials were held, the sweat house used by the tribesmen daily, and the caches where the products of the environment were stored. The Yokaia of Ukiah Valley burned all the houses in the home village every spring and built temporary camps elsewhere. Each camp was established at a particular food source, one for acorns, another for buckeyes, and still another for fishing and seed gathering. The practice, of course, was unique although the Pomo of other village communities did burn their houses following a tribesman's death.

The Pomo lived in a world of supernatural beings and spirits. Coyote, the Creator, his grandsons Moon Hawk and Sun Hawk (the latter brought light to the world), Kuksu, the healer, and Gilak, the birdlike creature who searched the earth for bodies to devour, were among them. Evil spirits could be found in every spring, crevice, cave, and near every mountain top in the Pomo country. Charms, worn in the form of amulets, might ward them off; so might the taking of angelica.

The spirits were deeply involved in Pomo ceremonialism. Many were impersonated in the so-called *Kuksu* cults. Kuksu himself, for example, was represented by the wearing of a large feathered-stick headdress radiating from the wearer's head. In a ritual that lasted six days a series of dances and dramatizations were performed. Neophytes were "slain" symbolically by stabbing and were only "resurrected" through the wiles of the spirits. The Ghost Ceremony and the expulsion of Sahte, or the routing of the Devil, were other significant Pomo ceremonials. All served educa-tional functions. They were the means through which the young learned Pomo ways. By learning much a young man might one day even become a shaman.

For the young woman the outlets were different. While her chief tasks involved caring for the children, gathering and preparing foods, and making clothing, her talents could likewise be demonstrated in the arts. For she, like her mother before her, could aspire to be the finest of basket makers. From the willow used as warp and the roots of sedge, bulrush, digger pine, and the bark of the redbud used as woof, Pomo women manufactured their unique coiled and twined baskets. The women took special pains with design and decoration. Never did a design completely encircle a basket. A break was left purposely, for if it was not, the maker, the Pomo thought, would become blind.

The Pomo world was shattered for all time with the coming of the white man. While Spanish and Russian contacts made little impression, the American impact following the California gold discoveries (1848) was all-consuming. White settlers pushed into the Clear Lake and Russian River areas. They cleared acreages for orchards and crops. They destroyed the natural vegetation, the chief source of Pomo life. Pomo numbers declined rapidly. When in 1856 a reservation was created for them on the California coast they retired to it reluctantly. In 1868 when the reservation was abolished the Pomo returned to Clear Lake and Russian River only to find that the land was no longer theirs.

Today Pomo still live in the Clear Lake-Russian River homeland on government-purchased or privately owned land. There yet remains a Pomo group at Stewarts Point. The entire Pomo population numbers little more than 1,000. But who shakes the acorns loose from the tall oaks today? Whose nimble hands twine the beautiful Pomo basket?

lawmaking body. Each town, however, did have a headman — a chief. At Oraibi the chieftainship was held by the leader of the Bear clan who kept in his possession the sacred stone brought from the underworld by *Matcito,* the town's founder. During Soyal the chief was expected to display the stone, thus reaffirming his right to the chieftainship, and to the ownership of Oraibi lands. For here the clans held the land only on their good behavior and the proper observance of the ceremonials. The chief was regarded as the father of his people for he was concerned only for their welfare. He was the supreme authority in settling land disputes. The Hopi towns also had war chiefs. But other political functions were the responsibility of the clans.

Hopi leadership was able to cope with Spanish, Mexican, American, and other Indian incursions through time. It had always been the Hopi against the world outside. In the late 19th and early 20th centuries, however, events were moving too quickly for the calm Hopi. They would lead ultimately to the development of opposing factions within the neatly woven Hopi fabric. The Navajo began to plunder the Hopi fields, they stole their women and children, and they grazed their animals on Hopi lands. To forestall the march of the Navajo and perhaps to prevent the southward moving Mormons from settling in the Hopi country, a 3,900-square-mile reservation was created for the Hopi by executive order in 1882. The Hopi agency and a federal school had earlier been built at Keams Canyon. The Atlantic and Pacific Railroad — more than 60 miles south of the Hopi towns — also brought outside influences to the tribe. In 1893 H. R. Voth established a Mennonite mission at Oraibi. He had arrived during the rising tide of Oraibi dissension. There were those at Oraibi who bitterly opposed the coming of the white man (Conservatives); there were those who were friendly (Liberals).

When the government applied pressure upon the Hopi to send their children to the Keams Canyon school the Conservatives refused. They confined the Liberal leader, Lololoma, to a kiva; he was only rescued through the efforts of the United States Army. The Conservatives also disrupted the efforts of a United States survey to map the Hopi country. The factions grew completely irreconcilable. So great was the discord that two distinct sets — never complete — of ceremonies (including Soyal) were held at Oraibi between 1899 and 1906. The factions could no longer contain themselves. The battle was on. In a push-of-war (a goal line was drawn just outside of Oraibi) the Conservatives lost. As a result 300 members of the Conservative faction abandoned Oraibi and founded the new town of Hotevilla, seven miles to the north. Oraibi's population was further depleted when New Oraibi was founded at the foot of Third Mesa and Moenkopi (on the Navajo Reservation) was occupied.

Hopi dissension did not end in 1906. It reared its ugly head once more in the years following World War II. Many returning veterans found the reservation atmosphere stifling. They saw the need for better housing, the use of electricity, improved sanitation, and the betterment of general living conditions. But their views ran counter, of course, to the town elders who saw the "new" as a threat to the Hopi lifeway.

It has always been so — the conflict between the old and the new. Perhaps it will always be so. How do the more than 5,000 Hopi feel today about the influence of their Tribal Council, about the U.S. Public Health Service Hospital at Keams Canyon, about a water supply to the mesa tops and about the passing of the multi-storied pueblos? The new comes but the old lingers. The Soyal Kachina still staggers across the plaza at Oraibi at the approach of the winter solstice.

Zuni

Southwest Desert

The *Seven Cities* were part of the lore of Iberian Europe. They were given credence in New Spain by Nuño de Guzmán's slave, Tejo, who informed the governor that as a youth he had traveled north with his father, a trader, who had exchanged fine feathers in the Seven Cities for ornaments of gold and silver. The cities, he pointed out, were comparable in size to those in Mexico; their avenues were filled with the shops of silversmiths. The tale, of course, was widely circulated. It certainly inspired the expeditions of Guzmán (1529) and Fray Marcos de Niza (1539) to the north country. Fray Marcos is reputed to have seen the "city" of Cibola (probably the pueblo at Hawikuh) from a nearby height. He undoubtedly described it in glowing terms upon his return to Mexico. The following year (1540) Coronado, responding to the lure of the Seven Cities, started north. His crossbowmen and musketeers may well have stormed the Hawikuh pueblo. In a letter to the viceroy Coronado described the Seven Cities. Hawikuh (he called it Granada), for example, contained 200 houses of three, four, and five stories, all made of stone. Ladders were used to move from one story to another. The city was surrounded by a wall. Its people purchased cotton from distant neighbors (the Hopi), and they found fine salt crystals in a nearby lake. Cibola? — the Spanish corruption of Shi'wona, "the land that produces flesh." Coronado had found the Seven Cities of Cibola — the pueblos of the A'shiwi, "the flesh," the Zuni.

The Zuni had built their pueblos (save for Hawikuh) along the watercourses in the rough and all-too-dry country west of the Zuni Mountains. From the pueblo roofs the Zuni Buttes could be seen in the distant northwest; three miles to the southeast Taaiyalone Mountain, the beautiful red and white sandstone mesa — a Zuni refuge — towered over the landscape. It was to Taaiyalone that the

Zuni evacuated their women and children, as well as their property, prior to Coronado's assault. They were to return to the mountain in 1632 after the murder of the Franciscan missionaries (the first had arrived in 1629), again in 1680 at the time of the Pueblo Revolt (they remained until 1692), and in 1703 after the killing of the mission priest. At the time of the Pueblo Revolt there were but three Zuni towns; following the revolt a single new pueblo was built (population 2,500) on the north side of Zuni River, where the present-day village lies.

The Zuni were basically floodwater farmers. Long before the cloudbursts of summer the men of the households were in the arroyos clearing brush and building earthen dams to hold the water in check. They planted deep (in May) with the aid of digging sticks; they carefully weeded the fields with wooden hoes; they harvested the maize, squash, and beans (September or October), dried them on their flat roofs, and stored them in the inner recesses of the pueblo. The women, too, were part-time agriculturalists. They planted vegetable crops (tomatoes, onions, chili peppers) in small shallow rectangular depressions separated by hillocks of soil and nourished them with water brought from the river in pottery ollas. To supplement the vegetable diet the men hunted rabbits while the women gathered wild fruits, piñon nuts and seeds.

But the fountainhead of Zuni life lay not in the means of livelihood but rather in a sophisticated religious system that had evolved through the centuries. It was a system based upon ancestor worship — ancestors often identified with clouds and rain. Every Zuni had the right to pray to his ancestors. At the same time there developed a number of specific cults devoted to the worship of particular supernatural beings. Each had its own priesthood, its own rituals, its own fetishes, meeting places, and calendar of events. Of special significance was the Cult of the Sun. For the Zuni saw the sun as the source of all life. The *Pekwin,* or Sun Priest, therefore, was the most revered being in Zuni, the one chiefly responsible for the welfare of the pueblo. Other cults included the *Uwanami,* or "rain makers," the Kachinas, the Kachina priests, the War Gods, whose Bow Priests protected the pueblo, and the Beast Gods, made up of twelve medicine societies, each of which had a well-developed ritual of its own. The cults were virtually inactive in spring and summer but sprang to life during fall and winter.

The ceremonial season reached its climax in the *Shalako,* the all-pueblo house-blessing ceremony performed at the winter solstice. The Shalako were impersonators of the gods — their masks were long-haired, bearded, and great-eyed; they stood ten feet tall. They towered over the clowns, flute players and Bow Priests who conducted their approach to the pueblo. Upon arrival the Shalako

consecrated the new or recently built homes; they offered prayers for prosperity, fertility, long life and happiness. They led the Zuni in dancing and feasting. The Shalako exercises should be understood as something more, however, than mere annual ceremonials. They should be understood as symbols of the cohesion of a remarkable people who through time have withstood Indian contacts and threats, Spanish violence, the forced relationships of Catholic and Protestant missionaries, the rule of Mexico, and the all-consuming power of the United States. Through it all they have retained their composure, their strength, and their identity.

That is not to say that change has not come to the Zuni. For it has. The old site on Zuni River still contains the Zuni community. A cluster of flat-roofed, apartment-type dwellings remains. But all of the new homes (made of quarried stone or cement blocks and having pitched roofs) have been built on individual lots. Glass has replaced the clear sheet mica formerly used in the windows. TV aerials dot the community area. Trucks and cars are everywhere to be seen. The Zuni are served with electric power and a modern water supply. The women water pot carriers are no more. The farms are cultivated by machine; the women's supplementary gardens are all but gone. And population is growing. Over 5,000 Zuni live today on the old pueblo site and in the small summer farming communities at Tekapo, Pescado, Nutria, and Ojo Caliente. In the developmental area at Blackrock, in their elementary schools and at the Zuni High School the Zuni can look to the future. But in their language, their history, their rich religious and ceremonial life — the Zuni look toward Taaiyalone—and in the performance of the Shalako, the Zuni have an intimate tie with the past. Janus-headed, the Zuni can look backward and forward today without trepidation.

Navajo

Southwest Desert

Navajo chanters point out that the "First People" came to earth in the *Dinnetah,* the "land of the people," just east of the present-day reservation. There the first miracles were performed. There Ever Changing Woman, nourished on Huerfano Mesa, married the Son who sired the twins Monster Slayer and Sired-by-Water. Armed with swords of straight and jagged lightning the twins set about to destroy the monsters of the earth. They killed the man-eating eagle whose stone body we now know as Shiprock; they destroyed Ye'iitseh, the giant who devoured men whole (the flow of his blood can be seen today in the black lava near Mt. Taylor); they slaughtered the Rock Swallows, the Cutting Reeds, and the man-killing bear of Chaco Canyon. Aided by Spider Woman, Gopher, Big Fly, and Bat Woman, all of the monsters were slain — all save Poverty, Sickness, Old Age, and Death, who were permitted to live to keep man wide-awake and ever vigilant.

Mythology, it would appear, established Navajo beginnings in the American Southwest, perhaps in the wild country of north central New Mexico. Anthropologists and linguists, of course, have reached a rather different conclusion. They have traced the Navajo and their Apache neighbors through their Athapascan (or Athabascan) tongue to the Alaskan-Canadian north. They have learned that the Athapascan-speakers were late comers to North America; that they evidently crossed Bering Strait only 5,000 years ago. By 2000 B.C., however, Athapascan remnants had already given rise to the Tlingit and Haida and later Athapascans were to find homes in Oregon and California. Small Athapascan bands (hunters and gatherers), moving south by way of the Rocky Mountain frame, the Great Basin and/or the Great Plains, had reached the northern pueblo area (Colorado) by 1000 A.D.; they may well have contributed to the northern pueblo

demise. It was not until the 15th century, however, that the Athapascans, now the Apache-Navajo, wandered into the Dinnetah.

The Apache-Navajo ranged widely over the Dinnetah. They were familiar with the pueblos on the Rio Grande and with the Hopi villages. They raided the pueblos for maize, perhaps for women. They traded animal skins and meat for vegetables. In time, as a result of pueblo contacts, they began to plant crops themselves. When Fray Alonso de Benavides appeared among them in 1630 the Apache-Navajo were already successful agriculturalists. They lived in semi-subterranean dwellings and stored their harvests in small huts. They had well established trading patterns with the pueblos and had a strong feeling for the Dinnetah, a territory the Apache-Navajo considered their own.

Apache-Navajo contacts with pueblo peoples became even more intense during and immediately following the Pueblo Revolt (1680), for numerous pueblo dwellers fled to the Apache-Navajo for succor. The helpers, however, undoubtedly derived most from the contact. The Apache-Navajo refined their methods of floodwater farming, learned much about weaving and pottery-making, and acquired new skills in livestock care. They adopted many religious and social customs as their own: the use of masks, altars, the sand or dry paintings, the origin myth itself, and possibly the system of matrilineal clans. In casual raids against the Spanish settlements in the 18th century the Navajo (by then considered a distinct and separate group) secured livestock, horses, sheep, and goats all destined to change the Navajo lifeway markedly. During the same period Spanish missionary efforts at converting the Navajo to Christianity were somewhat less than successful. On the other hand many Navajo, particularly women and children, served Spanish masters as slaves. Only rarely, however, did the offspring of

slave-master unions return to the scattered Navajo settlements.

During the 18th century, too, the Navajo began to abandon the old Dinnetah. Mounted, and pushing their animals before them, they moved west into the plateau and canyon country of the present-day reservation. Their dispersed settlements, the forked-stick hogans, accompanying sweat lodges, ceremonial houses, dance grounds, and sheep corrals, their "doors" oriented to the sun, could be found near the Zuni country, in the isolated Chuska Mountains, in the steep-walled Canyon de Chelly, and in the country between. In the Canyon the newcomers took advantage of the floodwaters of two small streams to plant maize, beans, squash, and watermelons. They planted peach kernels (probably obtained from Spain via the Hopi) near the high cliffs (for protection from winds and for heat reflection) and watered them by hand. In all of the settlements the men did the farming,

the horse herding, and the little hunting that was done; the women, assisted by the children, cared for the goats and sheep.

The Navajo of the period were in no sense a tribe. The scattered settlements were completely autonomous. Each was led by a much respected individual, perhaps richer than the others, certainly wiser. He was expected to be a man of exceptional character, a fine orator; he had to be thoroughly familiar with the practical and religious aspects of Navajo culture, and to be in control of the ceremony called the "Blessing Way." The Navajo referred to him as *natani*. Each of the settlements also had a war leader, often several. In times of stress a number of the settlements might combine under the leadership of a particularly prominent natani or war leader but such occasions were apparently rare.

In the early 19th century the war leaders were kept particularly busy. Following a slave raid into Canyon de Chelly by the Spaniards

in 1804, in which many Navajo women and children were unfortunately slain, the Navajo took to the warpath. Armed with bows and arrows, lances tipped with Spanish sabers, protected by shields painted with magic symbols, and fortified through the spirits with the proper chants, the Navajo assaulted the Spanish settlements. And they continued to make their raids after the United States obtained control of Arizona and New Mexico in 1848.

Treaty after treaty made with individual natani did not stem the conflict. Fort Defiance was erected in 1852 in the heart of the Navajo country and it, too, was raided in 1860 by some 2,000 Navajo under Barboncito, Herrero, and Manuelito. Finally in 1863 General James H. Carleton and the territorial governor took it upon themselves to stop Indian raiding in New Mexico forever. They would round the Indians up, confine them to reservations, and teach them and their children the precepts of Christianity. By so doing, they thought, the Indians would become happy, contented, and above all peaceful. Kit Carson, field commander of the roundup, began his work by bringing in the Mescalero Apache. He then turned upon the Navajo. His strategy was simple: burn the cornfields, kill the sheep, and force the Navajo to come to Fort Defiance for food and clothing. While many Navajo fled to the pueblos, to the Apache, to the Supai and beyond, most gathered what belongings they could carry and moved into Fort Defiance. Then on March 6, 1864, the Navajo began their "Long Walk" — nearly 300 miles — to the "reservation," the Bosque Redondo on the banks of the Pecos. The walk was heartbreaking. The agony was to bite deeply into the Navajo soul. The Bosque Redondo scheme itself proved to be a complete failure. After four years of misery and privation the Navajo, 8,000 strong, were returned to their former homeland to begin life again. They set up new hogans and

planted anew. The Navajo began to work in silver, brass and iron. Navajo blankets became significant trade items.

Making the adjustments was not easy. For one thing the Navajo were increasing at alarming rates. The 8,000 who had returned from Bosque Redondo had become nearly 20,000 by the turn of the century, over 40,000 by 1930. The Navajo were then living in an overpopulated land, an eroding land, albeit accretions were made from time to time to the reservation. Observers urged erosion control, a better distribution over the reservation of the Navajo themselves, and a reduction in livestock. But the Navajo moved slowly. While they could see the need for livestock reduction, for example, they could not bring themselves to it. They could not at that particular juncture abandon their old ways and habits.

But change was to come to the Navajo all the same. Servicemen returning from World War II clamored for an expanded educational system. The Tribal Council began to recognize the fact that education was the prime need of the tribe. And there were others, as the Navajo-Hopi Long Range Rehabilitation Act (April 19, 1950) points out. Under the act over $88,000,000 was provided for school construction, hospital and health facilities, road improvement, irrigation construction, soil conservation, and the resettling of the Navajo off the reservation, if they so desired. As a result the Navajo have pushed themselves, and have been pushed, into the 20th century.

By 1960 oil was beginning to pour over $1,000,000 a month into the tribal coffers. Additional funds were accruing through the sale of coal, natural gas, and uranium. The Navajo were in school at Rough Rock and elsewhere. They had become wage laborers. But population was and is a threat. By 1960 there were over 73,000 Navajo. The present figure may be better than 90,000.

71

The Northern Tribes

The Northern Tribes lived near the coastal waters between northern California and southern Alaska, along Arctic Shores between the Aleutians and east Greenland, and in the Canadian Sub-Arctic from interior Alaska to coastal Labrador.

Migrants to the Northwest Coast adapted to an environment characterized by mild winters and cool summers, and replete with lush forests, fast flowing, salmon-bearing streams, and neighboring seas brimming with cod, halibut, and a variety of sea mammals. Northwest Coast culture waxed rich. It may well have reached its zenith with the Haida, the "Lords of the Coast," during the 19th century.

Along frigid Arctic Shores a different type of people, the Eskimo, made very different adaptations to varying environments. But everywhere the sea mammals, particularly the ringed seal, were the prime objects of the sea hunters. Everywhere, too, the Eskimo struggled with the cold Arctic winter, the "time of famine." And to survive in their severe Arctic environments they produced a life-giving inventory of ingenious inventions, the most significant of which, perhaps, was the harpoon.

In the tree-covered Canadian interior survival was also the focal point around which life revolved. The life-giver was the caribou or moose and the successful caribou or moose hunter was much honored in his band.

NORTHWEST COAST

The heart of the Northwest Coast culture lay in the far north where the Tlingit, Tsimshian, Kwakiutl and Haida spent their lives. There stood the gable-roofed houses facing the sea, the beautifully carved totem poles, the wooden boxes and implements, the sleek sea-going canoes. There the artist, like the shaman, the skillful harpooner, fisherman or sea hunter, was held in high regard. Society was stratified; it supported chiefs, nobles, commoners, and slaves. A prime attribute of the culture was the acquisition of wealth and its concomitant the *potlatch*—the ceremonial in which chiefs and nobles displayed and gave away their material goods. Potlatches were often held during the great life crises; they were held, too, to validate the donor's right to hold names and crests, thereby bringing honor and prestige to himself and his lineage.

Farther south, along the bays, rivers, and inlets of Washington, Oregon, and northern California the Northwest Coast culture was somewhat subdued. While the Chehalis, Chinook, Tillamook, Wasco-Wishram, Karok and Yurok displayed many traits typical of the northern tribes, a significant number of refinements were conspicuously absent. The villagers built gable-roofed houses but nowhere was a totem pole to be seen. They built fine canoes but none could match the majesty of the Haida vessel. They worked in wood and were fine artists but their skills did not achieve the beauty or perfection of the northern tribes. Here society was also stratified, with groups similar to the northern tribes. Gifts were given during winter ceremonials, but the true potlatch was unknown.

Numerous languages were spoken on the Northwest Coast, including Athapascan, Eyak, Salishan, Wakashan, Chimakuan, and Chinookan. Many were mutually unintelligible. Because trading ventures between the tribes were of marked significance a *lingua franca,* the Chinook jargon, came to be used as a trade medium. The "jargon" was considerably augmented when, in the 18th century, the European traders appeared on the Northwest Coast.

CANADIAN SUB-ARCTIC

In the Canadian Sub-Arctic, where trees, lakes and rivers were abundant, lived numerous Indian peoples. The eastern tribes, all Algonkian-speaking, included the Micmac,

Malecite, Montagnais-Naskapi and Cree; the western Athapascan-speaking tribes included the Chipewyan and Slave, the Yellowknife, Dogrib, and Kutchin. While most of the Canadian Sub-Arctic tribes were clearly addicted to the taiga and the hunting of the woodland caribou and moose, there were, too, the so-called "edge of the woods" peoples. These moved between the coniferous forest and the tundra, in search of the Barren Ground caribou, and therefore divided their existence between two worlds.

For most of the tribes home was a crude conical tipi covered with caribou hide or bark. The far western tribes often preferred single or double lean-tos made of a framework of poles covered with bark, hides, or brush. For transportation the canoe was everywhere significant; in winter snowshoes and the toboggan were employed. In the eastern portions the family hunting grounds were guarded zealously. Trespassers were often punished; leniency was only exhibited in cases of real need. The leadership of the individual bands devolved upon the most able hunter. It was he who could support a number of wives; he who could best bargain with the leaders of other bands; he who could best deal with the men of the Hudson's Bay Company when that enterprise became a prime factor in the country. The shaman, too, was everywhere important. And it is surprising, considering all the essential work she did, in a culture that was eternally bound by the food quest, that woman was held in such low esteem!

ARCTIC SHORES

The varied environments of the Arctic Shores and the culture contacts possible in each resulted in the somewhat differentiated cultural responses of the Eskimo. House types and art work may be used as cases in point. In the wood-free tundra west of Hudson Bay the Caribou Eskimo erected the domed igloo of snow blocks; in Greenland the igloo ground plan lay somewhere between circular and rectangular but the home itself was made of stone, whalebone, and sod; in Alaska, where wood was more plentiful, logs were used in construction. Log roofs were covered over with earth to provide proper insulation. On their travels in winter most Eskimo might build a temporary snow-block igloo; in summer they would rely upon the *tupik* or skin tent.

In art work the Alaskan Eskimo were clearly superior to their brethren across Canada and in Greenland. Through contact with the Athapascan Indians of the Northwest Coast the Eskimo learned the woodworking arts. They soon became proficient in bone, ivory and horn carving. Invariably they produced carvings of the sea mammals so well known to them — the whale, walrus and seal. They made and painted masks and carved the figures of dogs and bears. While the Eskimo west of Hudson Bay and in Greenland also engaged in carving, they simply produced fewer specimens, and their work was less noteworthy.

Considering, however, the immense area and the different environments inhabited by the Eskimo the culture of the Arctic Shores was remarkably uniform. The adaptation to the sea mammal was almost everywhere the same. The tailored clothing, including parka, fur stockings and fur boots, and even snow-goggles, was virtually universal. So, too, was the band organization. Almost everywhere he traveled — and the Eskimo was known for long distance sledge runs — he spoke a single tongue. Whether it was in East Greenland, or Ellesmere Island, near Coronation Gulf, on Barter Island, or north of Norton Sound he spoke Inupik; only south of the north shore of Norton Sound was Yupik the spoken language. And everywhere the Eskimo called himself *Inuit* — "humans" — "men."

73

Haida

Northwest Coast

The wind blows hard at Rose Spit. It has for centuries. But Raven of old did not mind the wind. From his home in the heavens he beat his wings. The nearby waters were wafted into the sky and were there transformed first into clouds and then into rocks. Raven watched as the rocks grew larger and larger under his eyes. He knew that they were soon to become *Lak Haida,* the rain-swept Queen Charlotte Islands. And to dwell among them Raven created the Haida people from a mound of clam shells. Thus a Haida myth records Haida beginnings.

Linguists, however, tell a somewhat different tale. Haida, they say, is a language related to Athapascan, Eyak, and Tlingit, which are Na-Dene tongues. Five thousand years ago Na-Dene was spoken in the Bering

Strait area. But as time went on and migrations took place the Na-Dene began to break up. Haida speakers, for example, probably diverged from the main line between 3,000 and 4,000 years ago. They undoubtedly became hunters in the Canadian interior. Sometime later their remnants (possibly moving westward by way of the Skeena River) appeared on the Pacific coast. They were already familiar with the canoe-building and fishing arts. At a still undetermined date they braved the open sea and the face-biting winds, sighted Rose Spit, and occupied Lak Haida. The Haida had arrived in a wet, water-girt land brimming with red cedar and teeming with animal, sea mammal, and fish life. Deer and caribou roamed the forests; halibut and cod swam in the open sea; salmon entered the fast-flowing rivers; and the sea otter swarmed in the coastal rookeries. Lak Haida was a veritable paradise.

The Haida soon became masters of their rich environment. They felled the red cedar and built their large, rectangular, gable-roofed houses — set side by side — on riverbanks or facing the open sea. Eighteenth century European explorers reported large poles standing directly in front of the Haida houses; access to an individual house was gained through an opening in the pole. In late spring and summer the abundant halibut were caught with hook and line. Women waiting on shore cleaned the fish, removed the bones, head, fins, and tail and cut the meat into strips which were placed on wooden racks and dried in the sun. The sea otter was pursued by a fleet of canoes, the herd surrounded and driven to exhaustion before Haida arrows completed their kill. In late summer and early autumn salmon were speared near river entrances or were trapped in weirs and netted. Salmon roe were deposited in wooden boxes and permitted to decompose. The same was often done with halibut and salmon heads. Haida delicacies!

To preserve their food the Haida used the oil of the *olachen,* or candlefish, obtained through trading expeditions to the Tsimshian country. In return the Haida offered red cedar canoes, beautifully carved wooden boxes, and dried halibut. In winter the Haida rested on their summer laurels; winter was a time for feasting, dancing, and producing fine art forms.

Because of the ever-present food supply, their own genius, and their ability to take advantage of opportunities the Haida waxed rich. They developed a social system based upon class and a hierarchy of wealth; their trade and slave-hunting expeditions carried their swift canoes as far south as Vancouver Island and Puget Sound; they devoted much time to various art forms and became excellent workers in wood. And the Haida self-image was extraordinary. They considered themselves Lords of the Coast.

But everyone in fact was not a lord. For Haida society was composed of nobles and chiefs as well as commoners and slaves. The nobles and chiefs inherited their positions; the inheritor in a chief's family could, therefore, be groomed for his eventual role and reared to fulfill the expectations of his lineage. The nobles and chiefs were the wealthy among the Haida, the possessors of valuable material goods — the finest canoes, totem poles, robes, wooden boxes and utensils, copper plates, fish and sea mammal catches, as well as the less tangible items (but to the Haida equally as significant), the names, songs, and crests of the noblemen deceased. They were the much-respected guardians and the protectors of Haida traditions.

The commoners, in the Haida sense, were only lesser noblemen. They participated fully in Haida life. They, too, possessed particular names and crests but their material wealth was much less conspicuous than that of the

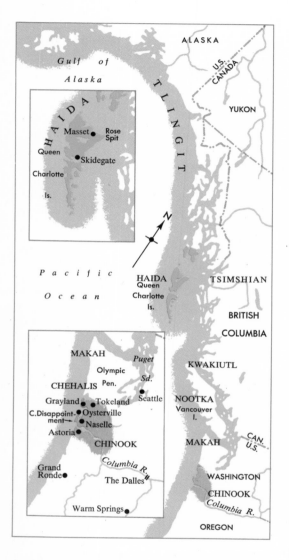

an heir, the marriage of a nobleman's child, or the death of a chief, Haida nobles invited their peers from, perhaps, another village to a *potlatch,* often called a "giving" ceremony. Here an Eagle or Raven (Haida moieties) nobleman might exhibit his prowess and wealth by giving away his material goods. The finest gifts would go to the highest ranking guests; the lesser gifts to nobles of lower rank. If the crest of an Eagle chief was passing to an heir its history was recited at length during the potlatch. Thus the ceremonial served to validate the fact that the crest had passed into new hands. While given by a nobleman or chieftain, the potlatch was in reality a community ceremonial. Everyone save the slaves was directly involved. As such, the potlatch was an important instrument in maintaining Haida solidarity.

In 1774 Juan Perez, the Spanish navigator, sailed north into Lak Haida waters inaugurating thereby Haida contacts with Europeans and the later American "Boston Men." After the Captain Cook expedition's successful run from the Northwest Coast to China the area (including the Queen Charlotte Islands) was besieged by numerous trading vessels pursuing the sea otter pelt. The Europeans and Americans came to Lak Haida as traders. They brought iron, copper and brass, muskets, powder and shot, beads, trinkets, and rum to the Haida villages. In return the resourceful Haida provided the white traders with animal pelts.

It is difficult to assess the impact of the newcomers upon the Haida world. But it does seem clear that the Haida bargained for those things they thought would help them most, those items which would fit well into their already established culture. Iron goods permitted them to fashion better chisels and other tools; canoes could be built with much less effort; totem poles could be made larger and more elaborate. Copper could be

nobility. Among them were the finest artists and canoe builders. A commoner might well be a young brother of a Haida chieftain. The slaves were often battle captives, chattels of the noblemen. They performed menial tasks in the Haida village and were virtually excluded from most facets of Haida social and ceremonial life.

On special occasions such as the birth of

Chinook

used for give-away items at potlatches; various cloths as trading goods.

The newcomers, however, brought with them alcohol, their guns, and particularly their diseases. Smallpox ran rampant through the Haida villages in the late 18th century as well as during the 19th century. Haida population, estimated in 1835 at over 6,000, stood at only 800 fifty years later.

Nineteenth century missionaries were witnesses to the population decline; they contributed, albeit unwillingly, to Haida demoralization. For example, when the Reverend W. H. Collison, an Anglican, arrived at Masset in 1876 he was made an Eagle; his wife and children became Ravens. Reverend Collison learned the Haida tongue and proceeded to perform his tasks as he saw them. The Haida must become civilized men. They must become people of the Book; they must no longer create graven images; no longer dance their primitive dances; they must abandon slavery and must give up the potlatch. And when the Haida became ill they must no longer accept the witchcraft of the shaman as medicine. The missionary impact upon the Haida was savage. It cut deeply into the fabric of Haida society. By 1915 Haida numbers were reduced to 588. The threat of extinction loomed as a possibility. But there has been a steady increase in population since the 1920's. In 1963 there were 1,224 Haida. The 1968 estimate for the two Haida villages, Masset and Skidegate, was 1,500.

At Masset the Haida are engaged in fishing as of old; they work in the peat moss industry and in construction. The women obtain seasonal employment at the crab cannery. At Skidegate the Haida still pursue the halibut and salmon. The Anglican Church remains at Masset; the United Church of Canada has helped to supply new vigor to Skidegate. But the old life is no more. The Eagle and the Raven cry.

Northwest Coast

The Columbia River threw sheets of white water across the sand bar and the ocean beyond churned. Chinook canoemen, for centuries aware of the treacherous shoals, maneuvered their craft with caution. They crossed the bar at high water and rode the sea, plying the merchant's trade, as far north as Vancouver Island. Their sleek canoes, brimming with trade goods, also found their way upriver to the great trading mart near The Dalles. But Vancouver Island and the The Dalles were part of alien worlds. The real Chinook homeland lay in the quiet waters behind the Columbia River bar, along the seacoast and bays north of the river, and along the lower river's north shore.

There the Chinook set up their small independent villages, built their cedar-plank houses, fashioned their sleek canoes, their watertight hats and baskets, their elk-skin arrow-proof armor. There the women, often accompanied by their slaves, combed the low marsh country for the wapato root and strawberry. There the men gathered clams, crabs, and mussels from the beaches and pursued the oyster. When time permitted they hunted the deer, elk, and black bear.

There the villagers pressed their babies' heads between wooden boards — artificially flattening the young skulls, a mark of those born free as well as a sign of beauty. There the shamans conversed with the good spirits attempting to destroy the influences of the bad. There the Chinook gambled and laughed their evenings away. There they were born, there they passed to adulthood, purchased their brides, and there after a full life they hoped to die.

In the late spring, however, the tribesmen left the quiet waters, often abandoning their villages *in toto*. They moved upriver to the churning water — the cascades — where salmon-catching was best. There they built temporary dwellings and huge drying sheds.

With dip net, seine, and spear they attacked the swarming salmon. During the opening ten-day period they caught, roasted, and consumed the salmon for it was taboo to store them. But the succeeding catches were dried and later sold or bartered along with other choice items at The Dalles emporium.

But the idyllic lifeway of the Chinook was sharply interrupted by the coming of the European and American explorers. Bruno Hecate had probably sighted the Columbia River bar in 1775. John Meares sailed into Willapa Bay in 1788 and actually made contact with the Chinook. Cruising south, searching for a protected cove or inlet, he found only a rocky promontory and a line of breakers. He named the promontory Cape Disappointment, an adequate expression of his feelings. In 1792 George Vancouver was in these waters. But it was left for Captain Robert Gray and his *Columbia Rediviva* to negotiate the crossing of the Columbia River bar and move into Chinookan waters. Thirteen years later Lewis and Clark were tramping over Cape Disappointment, and in 1811 John Jacob Astor's ship *Tonquin,* backed by a bracing ocean wind, passed the bar at the mouth of the Columbia River.

The men of the *Tonquin* established Astoria, on the south side of the river just opposite the largest Chinook village where Comcomly was *tye-yea,* or headman. Comcomly forged excellent relations with the new traders. So great was his zeal for the American cause that when the British sloop of war *Raccoon* appeared in Chinook waters in 1813, he appeared at the fort in full battle regalia with several hundred men at his back. Fortunately Comcomly was held in check by the fort's proprietors who watched quietly as the *Raccoon's* master raised the Union Jack. One-eyed Comcomly, whose daughter had married Duncan M'Dougal, Astoria's leader, gazed on in utter bewilderment. Surely the Americans, and his own beloved daughter, were now no better than slaves.

The Chinook, however, survived the coming of the American and British traders. Their own canoes continued to plow the sea and the river. They brought beaver pelts from The Dalles to Astoria, which was returned to the United States in 1818. They procured *dentalia* shells and sea otter pelts from the northern markets. And it was their language — Chinookan — which contributed the greatest number of words to the *lingua franca* of the entire Northwest Coast, the so-called "Chinook jargon."

In 1829, however, the "ague fever," of unknown origins, swept the lower Columbia River. Entire villages were wiped out. The Chinook never really recovered. Their population, estimated in 1805 at over 400, was reduced to 112 in 1885. And no longer were they the Chinook of old. The shattered remnants of 1829 had consolidated their villages, intermarried with European and American settlers, and were virtually fused with their neighbors, the Salish-speaking Chehalis whose language they adopted. When Major John Wesley Powell made his population estimates of the Indian tribes in 1885 he found over 500 Chinook, many of them isolated remnants in alien lands, on the Warm Springs, Yakima, and Grand Ronde reservations in the states of Oregon and Washington.

In the quiet waters behind the Columbia River bar few Chinook remained. Today many small towns, Oysterville, Nahcotta, Naselle, Tokeland, Grayland, sit on old Chinook village sites. Ilwaco bears the name of an old Chinook chief. But Comcomly's village site has been washed by erosion into the river. You are not apt to hear the trader's cry in Chinookan waters today, but if you look hard enough you may well find a Chinook — certainly a man, who in his pride, calls himself one.

Chipewyan

Chinook

Chipewyan

Canadian Sub-Arctic

In the Sub-Arctic the Chipewyan pursued the caribou. They speared them in lake and river on the Barren Grounds in summer, and drove them into pounds or corrals, making their kills with bow and arrows amid the cone-bearing trees, in winter. When caribou were scarce, in near-famine years, they hunted the musk ox or moose, and trapped the wolf, Arctic fox, lynx, and marten. They snared ducks, caught a myriad of salmon and smelt with spear, bone hook, or net of babiche, and gathered mussels, crabs and starfish on Hudson Bay beaches. They captured geese in the marshes and devoured the flesh of partridges, owls, and hawks. They knew intimately the face of the land between Chesterfield Inlet and the eastern ends of Great Slave Lake and Lake Athabasca south to Churchill River.

On summer treks their small bands came into intimate contact with other tribes or peoples: Eskimos on the east and north; Crees on the south; and Dogribs and Yellowknives on the western flanks. From the Eskimos they learned to use the double-bladed paddle and perhaps to eat raw meat and fish; the Crees taught them to make birchbark vessels in which food could be boiled; from the Dogribs and Yellowknives they learned to tattoo their faces; from the Yellowknives, who themselves learned it from the Eskimos of the Coppermine River, the use of copper for knives, awls, hatchets, and arrow- and spear-heads.

But the borrowings took place on the fringes of Chipewyan territory; in the interior life went on as it had for centuries. Man provided the sustenance for family and band; woman the everyday toil. It was she who lugged food, hides, and household goods on her back across the Barren Grounds in summer; she who dragged heavy toboggans and sledges over the deep-lying snow in winter. It was she who brought up the young, who

source of food, to be holy. They envisaged a big white mountain made of caribou hair, called Caribou House, in which thousands upon thousands of caribou lived. They knew it was *Atikwapeo,* or Caribou Man, who presided over Caribou House. They knew it was he who made arrangements for the annual migrations. They knew it was he who directed the caribou to meet the proper Naskapi hunters who themselves had dreamed of such occasions.

In late summer near where the Larch River becomes the Koksoak the Ungava band set up their caribou-skin tents. When the caribou moved into the water, and they did so in droves, the Ungava surprised them in their two- and three-place canoes. They drove them toward shore and the campsite. Knowing that the caribou could be brought to earth only if the animals were prepared to submit to their weapons, the Ungava made their spear thrusts with great trepidation. But the kills were often many. Caribou carcasses were stripped of skin and fat. The meat was subjected to hot smoke, dried, and stored. Occasionally, after prolonged periods without food, the Ungava gorged themselves with caribou meat.

The Ungava slaughtered ptarmigan by the thousands and used their feathers for decorating their clothing and hair. They netted or hooked the salmon, trout, sucker and whitefish. They hunted the lynx, the hare and porcupine, and occasionally netted the beaver. Wolf, fox, and wolverine were killed but never eaten. The wolverine, considered a mischief-maker, was often tortured and tormented. Farther south, in the forested country, moose and beaver replaced the caribou as the chief food source, and the bear was the chief object of Naskapi ceremonialism.

In the 17th century European traders had ventured into Naskapi country. Traders and priests both ministered to the nomads. But the most dramatic influences upon Naskapi

life were to come later. In the second-quarter of the 19th century Hudson's Bay Company posts were set up at choice points: Ft. Chimo, on the right bank of the Koksoak, at Whale River, at Nichicun (Nitchequon), and at Ft. Nascaupee on Lake Petitsikapau, among others. The Naskapi bands began to make the annual trek to the posts. They bartered their pelts for guns and ammunition; flour, peas, beans, rice, and sugar; for cloth, beads, and needles; for molasses and tobacco. They mixed molasses, tobacco and water to make a drink which thoroughly stupefied them. The Naskapi longed for it.

By mid-19th century the Montagnais-Naskapi numbered about 2,500. By that time the bands had rooted themselves in definite land tracts. But the bands were quite small. The Moisie numbered only ten families who lived on either side the height of land; the Petitsikapau could count but six family heads; the Nichicun numbered 87 in 1857 but by 1925 only eight families remained at the old station; the Ungava, a relatively large band, was struck by a famine in 1892-1893, when the caribou did not emerge from Caribou House, and Ungava numbers dipped from 350 to less than 200.

In the 1950's, with the exploitation of the rich Labrador iron ores, the town of Schefferville was founded deep in Naskapi country. A rail line linked Seven Islands on the St. Lawrence River, with the new mining town. French Canadian, British, French, Italian, Portuguese and American immigrants moved to Schefferville. Among the newcomers were the Montagnais who settled on a ridge near John Lake. In the summer of 1956 the Ungava band of Naskapi, 200 strong, trekked south to settle at the base of the same ridge.

In winter the wind still howls and the snow piles deep across the Labrador-Ungava peninsula. But for the Naskapi life will never be the same again.

82

Eskimo

Arctic Shores

In the farthest north the Eskimo faced frigid but relatively hospitable Arctic waters. In western and northern Alaska, on the shores of Coronation Gulf and the islands to the north, and along Greenland's icy coasts the Eskimo stared seaward. For the friendly sea brought the sea mammals: the life-giving ringed, bearded, and harbor seals; the walrus; and the bowhead, beluga and North Atlantic right whales.

The virtually non-migrating ringed seal, known from the Bering Sea to northernmost Greenland, was patiently awaited in dark winter at breathing holes in the ice; in early spring the hunter approached his quarry, often basking in the sun, on the ice-covered sea near shore while he imitated its every move. During the open-water summer, pursuit was often made by *kayak,* the skin canoe utilizing a double-bladed paddle. For the kills, an ingenious weapon, the harpoon, was employed. Thrust into the body the harpoon head locked itself toggle-like in the seal's flesh. The attached sinew line served to buoy up the body and the heavy sea mammal could not sink. From the ringed seal the Eskimo secured his choicest meat, a blubber that burned with little smoke and considerable heat, and light skins for clothing. The walrus furnished ivory for implements, hide for kayak covers, as well as meat and blubber. The whales offered baleen and oil.

In early summer when the tundra exploded in a profusion of plant life, the caribou was attracted north. The Eskimo, turning their backs to the sea, prepared for the coming. They lay in wait for the herds at river crossings; they set up converging rows of stones—often miles in length—to lure the caribou to given points; near Alaska's wooded areas they erected corrals, fortified them with stakes, and slung snares between them. During the autumn when the caribou's back lay thick with fat and his body smooth with hair, the Eskimo pressed their kills. Caribou skin was used for clothing, sinew for thread, fat, blood, marrow and meat for food, and antlers for bows. The Caribou Eskimo of the Barren Grounds used caribou tallow in their lamps. In varying locales other food sources included: mountain sheep, bear and moose, musk ox, wolf, fox, and wolverine, and a myriad of ducks, geese, ptarmigan, fish and even berries and roots.

But food was not often plentiful and the supreme test for the Eskimo was survival through the cold dark winter, the "time of famine." Therefore, the cache had great significance. Food was stored on scaffolds or rock piles, under beach rocks, in caves, or in deep trenches beyond the reach of dogs and other predators. On King Island in the Bering Sea, one large cave was used by the entire band. Individual caches, including the joints and carcasses of sea mammals, were marked with crude designs representing marks of ownership. Among the Copper Eskimo caches were family owned. To partake of a cache that was not one's own, unless starvation was a threat, was considered criminal. Other bands treated the cache as common property. If you came upon it in time of need it was yours to dispose of at will.

Eskimo culture did not burst into full flower on the Arctic scene without antecedents. Migrants from Asia, pushing eastward through Alaska, occupied portions of the Pacific littoral. The earliest occupations may go back 6,000 years or more. The evolving culture produced stone lamps, lances for whaling, the harpoon, and numerous slate blade forms. From their neighbors, the Indians of the Northwest Coast, the migrants may have learned to decorate their clothing, to work in wood, to paint and weave. Farther north, on the Bering Sea, the culture evolved somewhat later and somewhat differently. It was based upon exploitation of

whale, seal, and walrus. The houses were rectangular and subterranean. Walls and roof were made of whalebone, stone, and wood. The harpoon was developed and hunting was from kayak and *umiak,* the latter a simple single-paddle skin canoe. Assaults by land in the interior, by toboggan and sled, were made upon caribou and musk ox. For the men the bow drill, ice pick, adze, and whalebone shovel were particularly useful. The women stuffed needles in needle cases and used wooden buckets for storage. Farther east between Hudson Bay and Greenland — and even later in time (c. 800 B.C.)—still another tradition was evolving. Harpoons and burins appear in the earliest horizons (stone lamps and snow knives somewhat later) as these so-called Dorset folk pursued seal, walrus, and polar bear. Then the bearers of the Thule culture (prior to 1000 A.D.) began to spread eastward from Alaska to Greenland. They developed soapstone lamps and cooking pots, buckles and swivels for dog harnesses, and quite possibly the snow house and breathing-hole hunting which undoubtedly originated under the most severe Arctic conditions. From these vital beginnings did the culture of the Eskimo finally emerge.

Early European travelers in the tundra reported that the very same language (Inupik) was spoken by the Eskimo from Greenland to Alaska. Only south of Golovin on Norton Sound was the speech (Yupik) really different. Linguists and archaeologists, combining their talents, point out that the mother tongue, Eskaleutian, was in use well before 4000 B.C. Aleut apparently split from the parent language at an early date. Subsequently Yupik and Inupik were also separated. The bearers of the Thule culture undoubtedly carried Inupik on their eastward migrations all the way to east Greenland.

Erik the Red planted the first European settlements in southern Greenland about 980

A.D. Contacts between Eskimos and Norsemen during the following centuries may have been frequent. But by the 16th century all communications between Greenland and the outside world had ceased. In 1721 the Danish missionary, Hans Egede, found the long-abandoned Nordic villages along the coast. He set for himself the task of converting the nearby Eskimo populations to Christianity. Dutch, Danish, Scottish and later, American whaling vessels began to frequent Greenland's coasts. In 1818 Sir John Ross discovered the Polar Eskimo on Greenland's northwest coast. So deep was their isolation that they considered themselves to be the only people in the world. One hundred years later the Danes were operating a trading post at Thule on North Star Bay. The Polar Eskimo would be isolated no longer. During World War II Denmark granted the United States the right to build weather stations and air bases in Greenland. Following the war the bases at Söndre Strömfjord, Narssarsuak, and at Thule continued to be used. *Greenlanders,* as they prefer to be called — they are largely a Danish-Eskimo mixture — helped to maintain the bases. They can be seen today fishing for cod, working in the shrimp canneries and filleting factories, or in the mines, or going to school.

Europeans arrived in Alaska much later than in Greenland. Russians, for example, were in Aleutian waters only by mid-18th century. They came to pursue the sea otter and seal. Their impact upon the Aleut and neighboring Eskimo populations was devastating. The natives succumbed to both murder and disease. The Eskimo of Northern Alaska were spared the devastation. They were not seen by outsiders until Sir John Franklin and Captain F.W. Beechey appeared in the Chuk-

chi and Beaufort seas in 1826. Significant contacts, however, did not take place until the coming of the whalers after 1848. For sixty-odd years the whalers plied Alaskan waters. They brought liquor, guns, matches, molasses, metal goods and tobacco to the Eskimo villages. The repeating rifle wrought havoc with the subsistence economy; whiskey brought demoralization; and diseases such as measles, influenza, smallpox, and tuberculosis often caused death. Under American tutelage (Alaska had been purchased in 1867) schools were brought to the north; medical missionaries ushered in a new era in Eskimo medicine; and reindeer herds were introduced from Siberia to aid the economy. The original purchase of one hundred seventy-one reindeer in 1892 was augmented by 1,280 during the next decade. By 1930 the herd was estimated at over 600,000. Unfortunately the numbers have dwindled in more recent years — to 200,000 in 1940, to a mere 50,000 in 1950. Parasites, wolves, inadequate tending by Eskimo herdsmen, overgrazing and perhaps the inability of the sea hunters in general to cope with herding routines caused the reindeer's demise. At Point Hope the herders would return to the village to participate in spring whaling activities; it was then that the reindeer strayed from the fold.

Since the 1920's much emphasis has been placed upon wage labor. Discoveries of oil following World War II, the growing work of the United States Coast and Geodetic Survey, and the establishment of the DEW line (1953-1957) have brought high-paying jobs to the Eskimo. Sharp cuts in these activities would bring much stress to the villages. It may be that the Eskimo still has one leg in the aboriginal world, but he is certainly moving toward the future.

Epilogue

The American Indian: Retrospect and Prospect

American Indians have inhabited North America for perhaps 40,000 years. By 15,000 years ago the descendants of the first Americans had already pushed south into Venezuela and 8,000 years ago their encampments could be seen near the Strait of Magellan. Alaska, Michigan, Massachusetts, Arizona, Mexico, the Antilles, Peru, and Chile — the Indians had occupied the entire American landscape.

In so doing, of course, they had adjusted to, and in a sense conquered, the American earth. They had hunted mammoth and old bison on the Great Plains, hunted ground sloth and netted waterfowl in the Great Basin, ground acorns into flour in California. They had developed suitable institutions to meet peculiar needs in varying locales. Later, in southern Tamaulipas, in the Tehuacán Valley, in distant Peru, and probably in a number of other places, they learned to plant crops — from seeds in the north to roots in the south. And these plants were diffused far and wide. Maize, for example, found its way from Mexico north to New England and south to the Andes. It was to become a food staple in Mesoamerica, the southwest desert, and even in the northeast and southeast. It would become an important trade item in the hands of the Indians of the prairies. The Iroquois clans would consider it one of their "Three Sisters."

By the time of the European conquests the Indian cultures had become further diversified. There were Indian peoples such as the Maya, the Arawak and the Aztec who were well on the road to what we might call "civilization." There were those like the Hopi and the Zuni who lived in sedentary agricultural villages and engaged in floodwater farming. There were the fishermen, the gatherers, the hunters, the farmers, the "primitive," and the "civilized." All were to feel the barbed words, the marked "superiority," the cold steel of the Europeans. So egocentric was the Catholic view of the day for example, so distorted its vision, that the Papal Bull of 1537 finally had to concede that the Indian was in fact a human being, and since he was a human being he possessed an immortal soul.

Distorted views were also held by Protestant groups, by government officials and by literary men who often referred to the Indians as "savages," or "barbarians." For the infant government of the United States, and for succeeding governments as well, the Indian was a "problem," since Americans were either fighting their Indian neighbors or pushing westward into Indian lands. Indians and Americans, the distinction was real, were becoming increasingly involved with each other. How would Americans and American government, in the best democratic tradition, solve the so-called Indian problem?

THE NORTHWEST ORDINANCE (1787)

In the Colonial Period the views that intelligent men held were quite rational for their day. The Indians, albeit they were "savages," could certainly be brought out of their lethargy, could be persuaded to practice European ways, could be brought to the pinnacles of "civilization." They needed only the opportunities. Missionaries, educators, learned men in the professions, even governments, must persevere in showing the Indian the way. And the prevailing mood passed ultimately into a significant piece of legislation, known as the Northwest Ordinance (passed by the Confederation Congress), in which the dominant attitude toward the Indian was enunciated:

> The utmost good faith shall always be observed towards the Indians; their land and property shall never be taken from them without their consent; and in the property, rights, and liberty, they never shall be invaded or disturbed, unless in

just and lawful wars authorized by Congress; but laws founded in justice and humanity shall from time to time be made, for preventing wrongs being done to them, and for preserving peace and friendship with them.

THE INDIAN REMOVAL ACT (1830)

But the mood of the Ordinance was not long to remain. The land hunger of white Americans was to prove too strong. And Americans could solve a vexing problem with an easy solution. Explorers in the trans-Mississippi west had reported with some finality that western lands would never be useful to white Americans, yet because of unlimited game (particularly on the plains) the lands of the west might be more than a suitable home for the Indians. Why not send the Indians west where they would forever be safe from the encroachments of the white population? John C. Calhoun, Secretary of War, outlined such a plan in 1825. He had urged it upon President James Monroe, who, in turn, urged it upon the American Congress. The removal of the Indians became only a question of time and circumstances.

President Andrew Jackson, a willing adherent to the removal policy, finally signed the Indian Removal Act (May 28, 1830). The Act was a discretionary one. It authorized the President to make treaties with the eastern tribes, to make payment for the lands vacated, and to purchase new lands for the Indians in the west. When the Cherokee and Seminole refused to sign a treaty and refused to move, they were answered with the United States Army. General Winfield Scott with 7,000 troops began to round up the Cherokee. He was to provide the "protection" over the "Trail of Tears." The Seminole, of course, fought the armies hard. And while many of their number did eventually depart for Indian Territory, there were those who remained in the wilderness of south Florida. Their descendants remain there to this very day.

THE GENERAL ALLOTMENT ACT (1887)

Removal of many of the eastern tribes to western lands did not solve the so-called Indian problem. Nor did the creation of the reservations. White Americans moved into the western lands. They brought with them their notion of free enterprise, their idea of private ownership of land — concepts to which the Indian was not attuned. And the Indian would not bow to them. His world was still communally oriented; even the reservation belonged to "the people." But the lawmakers were adamant. Senator Pendleton of Ohio could proclaim:

They must either change their mode of life or die . . . we must change our policy . . . We must stimulate within them to the very largest degree, the idea of home, of family, and of property. These are the very anchorages of civilization; the commencement of the dawning of these ideas in the mind is the commencement of the civilization of any race, and these Indians are no exception.

The General Allotment Act, calling for the parceling out of tribal land to individuals in 40, 80, or 160 acre tracts (the notion was that they would be farmed) was passed February 8, 1877. Title to the land was to be held in trust by the United States for 25 years. Lands not allotted were to be declared surplus and opened to homesteading.

Allotment was carried out in reservation after reservation, often over the objections of the tribesmen. The Indians, unaware of the value of their acres, leased them to whites at low figures, passed them off to guardians, or were simply cheated out of them. The system was conducive to bribery and corruption. In the years between 1887 and 1930 the tribes under allotment lost nearly two-thirds of their land. And it became quite obvious that the General Allotment Act had not solved the Indian problem.

THE INDIAN REORGANIZATION ACT (1934)

Under President Franklin D. Roosevelt and his new Commissioner of Indian Affairs, John Collier, a "new deal" was presented the Indian in the Wheeler-Howard Act (1934), commonly called the Indian Reorganization Act or the IRA. The possibility of communal living (the Indian way) was the Act's underlying principle. Allotments were no longer to be made. The Indians were to act for themselves in their own best interests. Funds were provided for the purchase of new land, for improving schools, for individual loans. The Act provided that the tribes accepting it must conserve their soil, water, vegetation and timber. It offered jobs to Indians in the Bureau of Indian Affairs without regard to Civil Service laws. A related law (1935) encouraged a return, or a development, of many of the old cultural aspects such as the old religions, the ceremonials, the crafts.

Unfortunately World War II intervened. Funds were obviously poured into the war effort. Appropriations for the Bureau of Indian Affairs were cut. Many of the facilities on the reservations literally deteriorated. The World War II period was as the *Report of the Commission on the Rights, Liberties, and Responsibilities of the American Indian* suggests, one of ". . . very little advancement — if not, indeed, retrogression . . . ." The failures during World War II, of course, cannot be charged to the Indian Reorganization Act.

HOUSE CONCURRENT RESOLUTION 108 (1953)

In the late 1940's and early 1950's there was a growing interest in transferring Indian social programs from the federal government to individual state governments. House Concurrent Resolution 108 (1953), frequently referred to as the *termination* "law," provided for the end of federal supervision of the Indians in four states (California, Florida, New York, and Texas) and for five specific tribes (Flathead, Klamath, Menominee, the Potawatomi of Kansas and Nebraska, and the Chippewa of Turtle Mountain, North Dakota) in other states.

The Menominee and Klamath were quickly terminated, perhaps too quickly. The Menominee of Wisconsin, for example, numbering 2,500, were at termination ". . . ill-housed, underemployed, poorly educated, and, as it turned out, in poor health . . . ." They were expected to move ahead as quickly as possible toward self-government and self-support. The old reservation in Oconto and Shawano counties was made into Wisconsin's 72nd county and called, appropriately, Menominee. The Indians established *Menominee Enterprises* to control the local mill operations. Stock certificates and income bonds were issued to tribal members. The single corporation was forced to bear 90% of the total taxes for the new county. The going was difficult.

In 1955 a Menominee Indian Study Committee was established to study the problems of termination transition. Its ten-year report was published in 1966. It recommends the development of a long-range federal-state-county plan to bring the Menominee lasting economic and social stability. But the Menominee knew that the road ahead would be rocky indeed.

THE 1960's

It had become evident even before the 1960's that termination as such was not the solution to the Indian problem. Nor was it simply a matter of relocating in the large cities. It was still virtually impossible for the Indian to compete with the white man in the white man's world. The gap between Indian

INDIAN RESERVATIONS

Major Areas Under Some Degree
of Federal Responsibility — 1970

American and white American had steadily widened through the years.

President Lyndon B. Johnson's *Message from the President of the United States,* March 6, 1968, points out that the most striking fact about the American Indians today is their tragic plight :

Fifty thousand Indian families live in unsanitary, dilapidated dwellings — many in huts, shanties, even abandoned automobiles.

The unemployment rate among Indians is nearly 40 percent, more than ten times the national average.

Fifty percent of Indian schoolchildren, double the national average, drop out before completing high school.

Indian literacy rates are among the lowest in the nation; the rates of sickness and poverty are among the highest.

Thousands of Indians who have migrated into the cities find themselves untrained for jobs and unprepared for urban life.

The average age of death of an American Indian today is 44 years; for all other Americans, it is 65.

President Johnson indicates further that our goal must be:

A standard of living for the Indians equal to that of the country as a whole.

Freedom of Choice: An opportunity to remain in their homelands, if they choose, without surrendering their dignity; an opportunity to move to the towns and cities of America, if they choose, equipped with the skills to live in equality and dignity.

Full participation in the life of modern America, with a full share of economic power and social justice.

President Johnson proposed therefore "... a policy of maximum choice for the American Indian: a policy expressed in programs of self-help, self-development, self-determination." And *they* should prove to be the keys for American Indian development in the years ahead.

RECENT DEVELOPMENTS IN CANADA

On June 25, 1969, the Honorable Jean Chrétien, Minister of Indian Affairs and Northern Development, rose in Canada's House of Commons and presented a statement of policy concerning his country's Indian population. He said in part:

> Governments can set examples, but they cannot change the hearts of men. Canadians, Indians and non-Indians alike stand at the crossroads. For Canadian society the issue is whether a growing element of its population will become full participants contributing in a positive way to the general well-being or whether, conversely, the present social and economic gap will lead to their increasing frustration and isolation, a threat to the general well-being of society. For many Indian people, one road does exist ... the road of different status, a road which has led to a blind alley of deprivation and frustration. This road, because it is a separate road, cannot lead to full participation, to equality in practice as well as in theory.

To assist the Indians in achieving a fuller participation in the social and economic life of Canada the new policy proposes:

1. That the legislative and constitutional bases of discrimination be removed;

2. That there be positive recognition by everyone of the unique contribution of Indian culture to Canadian life;

3. That services come through the same channels and from the same government agencies for all Canadians;

4. That those who are furthest behind be helped most;

5. That lawful obligations be recognized;

6. That control of Indian lands be transferred to the Indian people.

Some changes could take place rather quickly; others might take longer. The provinces, analogous to the American states, could take over many of the central government's responsibilities. Funds could be provided for economic development and the Department of Indian Affairs and Northern Development could be phased out, perhaps in five years. For complete transition and for complete equality a generation or two might be necessary for the task.

Reminiscent of President Johnson's statement, Jean Chrétien concludes:

> A policy can never provide the ultimate solutions to all problems. A policy can achieve no more than is desired by the people it is intended to serve. The essential feature of the Government's proposed new policy for Indians is that it acknowledges that truth by recognizing the central and essential role of the Indians in solving their own problems. It will provide for the first time, a non-discriminatory framework within which, in an atmosphere of freedom, the Indian people could, with other Canadians, work out their own destiny.

The solution to the centuries-old Indian "problem" may at long last be at hand. It will lie in the final analysis not upon legislation, not upon funds poured into tribal coffers, not upon white man's whims, but rather upon the Indians themselves and the decisions that they choose to make. But the Indian does not live in the world alone. Long term solution will depend, too, upon the recognition that the Indian is a human being, like other human beings, and must be treated as such by his fellow man.

Further Reading

Brophy, William A. and Aberle, Sophie D., *The Indian: America's Unfinished Business,* University of Oklahoma Press, Norman, 1966.

Coe, Michael D., *The Maya,* Frederick A. Praeger, Inc., New York, 1966.

Coe, Michael D., *America's First Civilization,* American Heritage Publishing Co., Inc., New York, 1968.

Driver, Harold E., *Indians of North America,* 2nd ed., University of Chicago Press, Chicago, 1969.

Drucker, Philip, *Indians of the Northwest Coast,* American Museum Science Books edition — The Natural History Press, Garden City, New York, 1963.

Eggan, Fred and Swift, Harold H., *The American Indian,* Aldine Publishing Co., Chicago, 1966.

Ewers, John C., *Indian Life on the Upper Missouri,* University of Oklahoma Press, Norman, 1968.

Farb, Peter, *Man's Rise to Civilization as Shown by the Indians of North America from Primeval Times to the Coming of the Industrial State,* E. P. Dutton & Co., Inc., New York, 1968.

Hagen, William T., *American Indians,* University of Chicago Press, Chicago, 1961.

Jenness, Diamond, *Indians of Canada,* National Museum of Canada, Bull. 65, 7th ed., Ottawa, 1967.

Jennings, Jesse D., *Prehistory of North America,* McGraw-Hill Book Co., New York, 1968.

Josephy, Alvin M., Jr., *The Indian Heritage of America,* Alfred A. Knopf, Inc., New York, 1968.

Kelly, Lawrence C., *The Navajo Indians and Federal Indian Policy,* University of Arizona Press, Tucson, 1968.

Lowie, Robert H., *Indians of the Plains,* American Museum Science Books edition — The Natural History Press, Garden City, New York, 1963.

Oswalt, Wendell H., *This Land Was Theirs,* John Wiley & Sons, Inc., New York, 1966.

Reaman, G. Elmore, *The Trail of the Iroquois Indians,* Barnes & Noble, Inc., New York, 1967.

Sanders, William T. and Price, Barbara J., *Mesoamerica: The Evolution of a Civilization,* Random House, New York, 1968.

Spencer, Robert F., Jennings, Jesse D., et al., *The Native Americans,* Harper & Row, New York, 1965.

Spicer, Edward H., *Cycles of Conquest,* University of Arizona Press, Tucson, 1962.

Spicer, Edward H., Ed., *Perspectives in American Indian Culture Change,* University of Chicago Press, Chicago, 1961.

Steiner, Stan, *The New Indians,* Harper & Row, New York, 1968.

Thompson, Laura, *Culture in Crisis: A Study of the Hopi Indians,* Harper & Row, New York, 1950.

Wauchope, Robert, *Lost Tribes & Sunken Continents,* University of Chicago Press, Chicago, 1962.

Willey, Gordon R., *An Introduction to American Archaeology,* Vol. I, Prentice-Hall Inc., Englewood Cliffs, 1966.

Index

92